THE IMPORTANCE OF

Clara Barton

These and other titles are included in The Importance Of biography series:

Alexander the Great	Harry Houdini
Muhammad Ali	Thomas Jefferson
Louis Armstrong	Chief Joseph
Clara Barton	Malcolm X
Napoleon Bonaparte	Margaret Mead
Rachel Carson	Michelangelo
Charlie Chaplin	Wolfgang Amadeus Mozart
Winston Churchill	Sir Isaac Newton
Cleopatra	Richard M. Nixon
Christopher Columbus	Georgia O'Keeffe
Marie Curie	Louis Pasteur
Amelia Earhart	Pablo Picasso
Thomas Edison	Jackie Robinson
Albert Einstein	Anwar Sadat
Dian Fossey	Margaret Sanger
Benjamin Franklin	John Steinbeck
Galileo Galilei	Jim Thorpe
Martha Graham	Mark Twain
Stephen Hawking	H.G. Wells
Jim Henson	

THE IMPORTANCE OF

Clara Barton

by
Rafael Tilton

Lucent Books, P.O. Box 289011, San Diego, CA 92198-9011

Library of Congress Cataloging-in-Publication Data

Tilton, Rafael.
    The importance of Clara Barton / by Rafael Tilton.
        p. cm. — (The importance of)
    Includes bibliographical references and index.
    ISBN 1-56006-058-1 (alk. paper)
    1. Barton, Clara, 1821-1912—Juvenile literature.   2. Red
Cross—United States—Biography—Juvenile literature.
    3. Nurses—United States—Biography—Juvenile literature.
    I. Title.   II. Series.
HV569.B3T54   1995
361.7'634'092—dc20   94-38562
[B]   CIP
                                                                    AC

Contents

Foreword

THE IMPORTANCE OF biography series deals with individuals who have made a unique contribution to history. The editors of the series have deliberately chosen to cast a wide net and include people from all fields of endeavor. Individuals from politics, music, art, literature, philosophy, science, sports, and religion are all represented. In addition, the editors did not restrict the series to individuals whose accomplishments have helped change the course of history. Of necessity, this criterion would have eliminated many whose contribution was great, though limited. Charles Darwin, for example, was responsible for radically altering the scientific view of the natural history of the world. His achievements continue to impact the study of science today. Others, such as Chief Joseph of the Nez Percé, played a pivotal role in the history of their own people. While Joseph's influence does not extend much beyond the Nez Percé, his nonviolent resistance to white expansion and his continuing role in protecting his tribe and his homeland remain an inspiration to all.

These biographies are more than factual chronicles. Each volume attempts to emphasize an individual's contributions both in his or her own time and for posterity. For example, the voyages of Christopher Columbus opened the way to European colonization of the New World. Unquestionably, his encounter with the New World brought monumental changes to both Europe and the Americas in his day. Today, however, the broader impact of Columbus's voyages is being critically scrutinized. *Christopher Columbus,* as well as every biography in The Importance Of series, includes and evaluates the most recent scholarship available on each subject.

Each author includes a wide variety of primary and secondary source quotations to document and substantiate his or her work. All quotes are footnoted to show readers exactly how and where biographers derive their information, as well as to provide stepping stones to further research. These quotations enliven the text by giving readers eyewitness views of the life and times of each individual covered in The Importance Of series.

Finally, each volume is enhanced by photographs, bibliographies, chronologies, and comprehensive indexes. For both the casual reader and the student engaged in research, The Importance Of biographies will be a fascinating adventure into the lives of people who have helped shape humanity's past and present, and who will continue to shape its future.

Important Dates in the Life of Clara Barton

Clarissa Harlowe Barton is born in North Oxford, Massachusetts.	1821	
Begins teaching career in Oxford, Massachusetts.	1832-1834	Nurses her brother David.
	1839	
	1850-1851	Attends the Liberal Institute in Clinton, New York.
Starts free public school in Bordentown, New Jersey.	1853	
	1854	Begins work as only woman clerk in U.S. Patent Office, Washington, D.C.
	1861	Civil War begins.
Takes supplies to front in many battles; works as volunteer nurse and cook.	1862 1862-1863	Obtains pass to battlefront.
Starts work of finding missing soldiers; Civil War ends April 9.	1864 1865	Is appointed superintendent of nurses in a Union army unit.
Joins Franco-Prussian War relief.	1869 1870-1871	Sails for Europe for health; learns of International Red Cross.
	1873	Returns to United States to promote Geneva treaty.
Meets Julian B. Hubbell; begins work for Geneva treaty and Red Cross.	1876	
Does fieldwork: floods of Ohio and Mississippi rivers; Johnstown, Pennsylvania, flood; hurricane in South Carolina.	1881 1882 1882-1884	Directs aid to Michigan forest fires relief; founds American Red Cross.
		U.S. Congress ratifies Treaty of Geneva on March 16.
Writes *The Red Cross: A History*. Cuban relief for *reconcentrados* and American soldiers in Spanish-American War.	1895-1896 1898-1899	Goes to Turkey to provide relief for Armenians.
American Red Cross is investigated.	1902 1903	Is elected president of Red Cross for life.
Founds National First Aid Society.	1904 1905 1907	Barton resigns; *A Story of the Red Cross* is published.
Dies in her home, April 12, at age ninety.	1912	Writes *The Story of My Childhood*; visits cousin W. E. Barton in California.

In the Name of Rightness, Justice, and Mercy

The most timid of adolescents, Clara Barton, at age eighteen, set out as a teacher, beginning the first of three major careers. She would become famous for bravery on the battlefield and for courage before statesmen and presidents. The cause for which the shy Clara Barton came to act so fearlessly was timely care of wounded soldiers. The work she started in the United States is the American Red Cross.

The founding of the American Red Cross came as the crowning achievement of a woman with high ideals and intense energy. Some might say that this national volunteer society arose out of the opportunism of war. Others would say that it grew out of the realization that humanitarian action is most needed when dire events occur. Some might believe that the horrors of war would be rejected sooner if humanitarians did not try to help its victims. Before such notions stands the life of Clara Barton, whose heart went out to those in misery.

Since the International Red Cross was first conceived in Geneva, Switzerland, in 1863, the United States has entered into two world wars and many military actions. In the light of these events, Barton's work takes on added significance. It remains true today, as it was at the time of the first Geneva convention, that nothing on earth can stop armed conflict if the opposing parties do not voluntarily settle their dis-

Clara Barton did not let society's sanctions restricting women's careers prevent her from achieving her goal: to create the American Red Cross.

Red Cross nurses return from the Spanish-American War. The American Red Cross remains an invaluable organization, long after Barton created it.

putes by negotiation. But no one who prays for peace, relieves pain, or receives care in suffering denies that such care has the power to heal.

Already a pioneer in making her way as a woman, Barton set about her task with determination. To succeed, she had to change the firmly set minds of a series of men in the White House and in the Congress, whose policy was isolationism—the decision not to enter alliances with countries across the oceans.

When, in 1878, Barton first approached President Rutherford B. Hayes with the Red Cross proposal, there may have been no other American who so well understood the workings and importance of international law. There certainly was no man who thought it possible to reverse U.S. isolationist foreign policy as set in place by the Monroe Doctrine of 1823.

Barton's methods were those of generations of women before her—study, letter writing, innumerable conversations behind the scenes. She did not wait for women to win the right to vote or equal pay for their work. She provided the legwork, the handwriting, the hard-earned savings. She came back again and again, patient, determined, stronger than ever after a setback. Always grateful for the fates that brought her public support, she did not consider approval or a public mandate necessary when her cause promoted rightness, justice, and mercy.

This, then, was Clara Barton. And the organization she founded, the American Red Cross, continues today, in the interest of humanity. Following in the footsteps of its founder, it relieves human suffering, overriding all concerns of political alliance, racial bias, and religious affiliation.

Chapter

1 A Precocious Child in an Ambitious, Close-Knit Family

Clarissa Harlowe Barton was born on Christmas Day, 1821, in North Oxford, Massachusetts, a small town in hilly New England. For her parents, two brothers, and two sisters she was an additional Christmas present. The older children drew her into their circle with immediate affection.

From the beginning, Clara's world was shaped by an education-minded family. Dorothy, the oldest Barton daughter, born October 2, 1804, was already teaching in the Oxford school. Stephen Jr., born March 29, 1806, was interested in mathematics. He, too, became a schoolteacher.

Barton's brother Stephen was a schoolteacher and taught Clara arithmetic.

The house in North Oxford, Massachusetts, where Barton was born.

David was born August 15, 1808. When he finished school, he indulged his love for the pedigreed horses their father raised and drew his brother Stephen back to partnership on the farm. Sally, two years younger, was going on eleven when Clara was born.

Each one took a personal interest in Clara's formal education. Dorothy taught her spelling and made sure she understood what she memorized for the others. Stephen taught her arithmetic. David taught her how to throw a ball and ride

Clara's brother David was interested in breeding and riding thoroughbred horses, a hobby that his father taught him.

horseback. Sally helped her read maps and learn the names of countries, states, and capitals.

Clara's mother, Sarah Stone Barton, was descended from a family that had fought for independence in the American Revolution. Sarah's orderly ways and insistence on cleanliness influenced Clara. An excellent family manager, Sarah taught Clara to cook, sew, weave, garden, and make soap.

Military Influence

Capt. Stephen Barton had fought in the Indian wars with the famous Revolution-

Introduction to Horseback Riding

Clara Barton loved horses and all animals to her dying day. Her skill as a rider saved her life and the lives of many Civil War soldiers. In The Story of My Childhood, *published in 1907, she tells how her brother David taught her to ride horseback.*

"To say that David was fond of horses describes nothing; one could almost add that he was fond of nothing else. He was the Buffalo Bill of the surrounding country, and here commences his part of my education. It was his delight to take me, a little girl five years old, to the field, seize a couple of those beautiful young creatures, broken only to the halter and bit, and gathering the reins of both bridles firmly in hand, throw me upon the back of one colt, spring upon the other himself, and catching me by one foot, and bidding me 'cling fast to the mane,' gallop away over field and fen, in and out among the other colts in wild glee like ourselves. They were merry rides we took. This was my riding school. I never had any other, but it served me well. To this day my seat on a saddle or on the back of a horse is as secure and tireless as in a rocking chair, and far more pleasurable."

ary War general "Mad Anthony" Wayne. He had taken part in the battles that defeated the great Shawnee warrior Tecumseh. In August 1795 he was present when the Indians gave up a large part of the Northwest in the Treaty of Greenville. Now a farmer and horse breeder, Clara's father managed extensive property and was a school board member whose opinion was respected at North Oxford town meetings.

In the story of her childhood Clara recalls how she loved her father's war stories and acted out the battles with him:

> Every shade of military etiquette was regarded. Generals, colonels, captains and sergeants were given their proper

Sarah Barton, Clara's mother, taught Clara domestic tasks and the importance of cleanliness.

place and rank. So with the political world; the president, cabinet and leading officers of the government were learned by heart.[1]

After making sure young Clara knew that the cavalry rode horses and the infantry walked, Stephen Barton promoted his daughter to reciting the names of the generals and on to admiring military strategy and authority.

But it was the family dog, Button, who slept on Clara's bed and followed her everywhere. For, as she remarks in *The Story of My Childhood*, "being the youngest by a dozen or so years, of a family of two brothers and two sisters, I naturally lacked child playmates and was left much to my own entertainment."[2] Button was even part of her lessons in fractions. He immediately ate his piece of whatever treat she was sharing with him and her brothers and sisters. Then, when it became clear that Clara had not counted herself before cutting the little cake or cookie and passing it around, the dog never gave her back even a tiny bit. True to her father's values, she did not complain.

A Timid Personality

Like her father, Clara found it difficult to express her feelings. She developed an exaggerated concern about causing others to worry. Two early experiences contributed to her belief that her needs were a trouble to others. In her autobiography she recalls the day she almost caught a snake near their front porch. Her mother's fright upon learning of Clara's encounter with the snake scared Clara

Apprentice to a Painter

Clara could be very direct when she wanted to help her family. During the remodeling of the Barton home she became interested in the redecorating skills of Sylvanus Harris. In The Story of My Childhood, *she tells how she learned a skill she used later in teaching people how to rebuild after a disaster.*

"I gathered the courage to . . . address him: 'Will you teach me to paint, sir?' 'With pleasure, little lady, if mama is willing, I should very much like your assistance.' The consent was forthcoming, and so was a gown suited to my new work, and I reported for duty. I question if any ordinary apprentice was ever more faithfully and intelligently instructed in his first month's apprenticeship. I was taught how to hold my brushes, to take care of them, allowed to help grind my paints, shown how to mix and blend them, how to make putty and use it, to prepare oils and dryings, and learned from experience that boiling oil was a great deal hotter than boiling water, was taught to trim paper neatly, to match and help to hang it, to make the most approved paste, and even varnished the kitchen chairs to the entire satisfaction of my mother, which was triumph enough for one little girl. So interested was I that I never wearied of my work for a day, and at the end of a month looked on sadly as the utensils, brushes, buckets and great marble slab were taken away. There was not a room that I had not helped to make better; there were no longer mysteries in paint and paper. I knew them all, and that work would bring calluses even on little hands."

worse than her own danger. On another day her brother David momentarily left her alone in a strange house during a funeral, and she was frightened by a heavy storm. She pictured the rolling thunder as

a huge old ram, that doubtless upon some occasion had taught me to respect him, and of which I had a mortal fear. My terrors transformed those rising, rolling clouds into a whole heaven full of angry rams, marching down

upon me. Again my screams alarmed, and the poor brother, conscience stricken that he had left his charge, rushed breathless in, to find me on the floor in hysterics, a condition of things he had never seen; and neither memory nor history related how either of us got out of it.[3]

From this time on, like her soldier father, she schooled herself not to let her loved ones know her fears.

Her family's pushing her to achievement, and her desire to please them, caused Clara also to fear that she could never meet their standards. She remembered no time when she could not read. She could spell three-syllable words before she started school. Yet she worried that she was not doing well enough and told her family nothing about her fears.

Clara started going to school with David and Sally before she reached her fourth birthday, but had to stop temporarily when she became ill with dysentery and nearly died at the age of five. She finally regained consciousness and strength, and had a solid meal. Clara always remembered the joy of that first meal after her recovery. In her autobiography, she writes:

> I can see this meal as clearly as if it had been yesterday. A piece of brown bread crust, about two inches square, rye and Indian, baked on the oven bottom; a tiny wine glass, my Christmas gift, full of home-made blackberry cordial, and a wee bit of my mother's well cured old cheese. There was no need to caution me to eat slowly: knowing that I could have no more, and in dread of coming to the last morsel, I nibbled and sipped and swallowed till I mercifully fell asleep from exhaustion.[4]

Clara returned to school after she recovered from her illness. Between the three-month terms, summer and winter, were the vacations, filled with gardening, care of the animals, helping the neighbors, and riding horses in the fields. Stephen Jr. and David decided to buy a farm, and Clara visited them often. Clara's life "seemed very full for a little girl of eight years."[5]

At school Clara continued to progress in her studies, but her determination not to trouble anyone with her needs showed itself as extreme shyness. One day Sarah Barton noticed that her daughter's gloves were full of holes and asked why she had not asked for new ones. Clara had no answer; she simply cried. It was at this point that the family realized how shy Clara was when it came to the fulfillment of her own needs. They decided she should attend a boarding school. They thought that away from home, among strangers, Clara would overcome her shyness and fears.

Only Clara's strong will helped her to survive leaving home at the age of eight. The cold boarding school bedroom, the strangeness of being among so many young people she did not know, the huge classrooms, the worry over answering questions in front of other students—all these factors only worsened her fears. She became very thin and nervous. One day in history class she mispronounced the name of an Egyptian king. The students' laughter embarrassed her so much that she left the room and refused to return. Her father had to come and rescue her. The family then was forced to admit that the experience of being away from home had not cured Clara's shyness. It only made her less willing to speak up for herself.

Playmates for Clara

In 1830 the family situation changed. The Bartons moved to another farm with a larger house and took in a family of cousins whose father had died. Clara now had playmates, three boys and three girls near her own age. This adventuresome crew tramped through three hundred acres of swamps and woods and explored the barns. They crossed the shaky, fourteen-inch log bridge that spanned the creek. Stephen Jr. and David had purchased the family's original farm, erected a sawmill on the stream, and started a lumber business. The children climbed every inch of the mill and fearlessly rode the saw carriage over the raceway with its rushing millstream twenty feet below. Clara's horseback riding skills reached a level that none of the boys could match. No one, not even Clara, doubted her physical strength and endurance.

Clara enjoyed taking care of her pet dogs and cats and the horses she rode. She raised ducks and learned how to milk the cows.

Only two things that Clara wanted to do were denied her—learning to skate and learning to dance. Unwilling to accept her parents' decision that these activities were not proper for a Barton girl, she learned instead a hard lesson of obedience. While skating without permission, she was badly injured. Finally, unable to disguise the pain, Clara showed her family her bloody knees. She accepted the care of a doctor and was proud to hear it said that she had borne the dressing of her wound "like a soldier."[6] She had to sit with her feet up for three weeks. During this time, she read the entire *Arabian Nights*.

When Clara was eleven, she had her first experience of nursing. Her brother David hurt his back seriously when he fell from the roof while raising a barn. Before

The Bartons' second home, after they took in the six cousins who became Clara's constant companions. The larger house and grounds allowed Clara to keep a variety of pets.

Child Nurse

Clara's care of her brother David made a lasting impression on her. In The Story of My Childhood *she tells how she applied leeches for the bloodletting that was supposed to cure David's fever.*

"My little hands became schooled to the handling of the great, loathsome, crawling leeches which were at first so many snakes to me, and no fingers could so painlessly dress the angry blisters; and thus it came about, that I was the accepted and acknowledged nurse of a man almost too ill to recover.

Finally, as the summer passed, the fever gave way, and for a wonder the patient did not. No physician will doubt that I had given him poison enough to have killed him many times over, if suitably administered with that view. He will also understand the condition in which the patient was left. They had certainly succeeded in reducing his strength.

Late in the autumn he stood on his feet for the first time since July. Still sleepless, nervous, cold dyspectic [with bad digestion]—a mere wreck of his former self. None were so disturbed over his condition as his kind-hearted, and for those days, skillful physicians, who had exhausted their knowledge and poured out their sympathy and care like water, on the patient who, for his manliness and bravery, and for his suffering, [they had] learned to love with a parent's tenderness.

It now became a matter of time. They could only recommend; . . . and various methods of external irritation for the withdrawal of internal pain followed, from month to month and season to season."

his back healed, he developed a persistent fever, which the doctors treated with the remedy of the day. Believing the fever was caused by too much blood, they applied small wormlike creatures called leeches to suck the blood from the patient's veins.

Clara insisted on being David's nurse. She would not leave his bedside and became the only one who could soothe and comfort him. After two years, another doctor convinced the family to discontinue the bloodletting, as the treatment with leeches was called, and try his new remedy of drinking fluids and sweating in a "sweat box." David rapidly improved and became strong and energetic again.

Clara had learned the importance of looking for better ways to care for the sick, but she herself had not grown or gained weight. Without play or companions for two years, she felt more shy and timid than before.

Relieved of her nursing duties, Clara returned to school. Studies had always been easy for her, and all subjects excited her. She regained her strength by walking a mile to school every day. After a year she went on to take philosophy, chemistry, and Latin.

Clara soon became involved in other healthful activities. She and two friends, Martha and Eveline, arranged long horseback riding parties whenever they had time. Clara read poetry with her sister Dorothy, and especially enjoyed *The Lady of the Lake* by Sir Walter Scott. She began to develop skill in writing verses.

Clara's brothers, seeing that manufacturing was becoming more important in Massachusetts, sold their farms and added to their prosperous lumber mill a cloth factory, called the Satinet Mill of North Oxford.

The Satinet looms fascinated Clara, and she found enough nerve to tell her family that she wanted to weave. They were about to refuse her wish to work when Stephen Jr. insisted on letting her try. The senior Bartons gave in, and a special high platform was built that made Clara tall enough to operate the shuttle. She had worked for only two weeks, finishing just one piece of cloth, when a fire burned down the mill in three hours.

A Final Cure for Shyness

Separated from an enjoyable occupation, Clara retreated into her timidity. She began pasting mementos into a scrapbook, did needlework, read, and wrote poems. The family worried that she would never overcome her bashful ways. In *The Story of My Childhood*, Clara writes that her parents discussed her personality with a visitor named L. N. Fowler. His practice of a form of psychology known as phrenology was based on measurements of the size and shape of the skull. While talking with Mrs. Barton, Fowler stated his opinion that Clara would never lose her sensitivity or learn to "assert herself for herself—she will suffer wrong first—but for others she will be perfectly fearless."[7] Fowler told the Bartons that Clara had the qualities of a good teacher.

Fowler's observation of Clara's "fearlessness" was more accurate than anyone could have imagined at the time. Clara would become a teacher, but her great concern for others would be revealed not as a teacher but on the battlefield and in the offices of world leaders.

Chapter

2 A Successful Teacher Moves on to Washington, D.C.

The suggestion of the psychologist Fowler gave Clara Barton the courage to choose a career in teaching. She knew she would be a good teacher, for she had seen how her own teachers had made it possible for her to receive an education far above the other students of Worcester County, Massachusetts.

In response to a Massachusetts law requiring free education for all, the public schools in the state were expanding rapidly, resulting in a great demand for teachers. Barton decided to apply for certification, although she had very little time to review her studies. The school committee for District 9 administered her oral examination on May 5, 1839, found her qualified, and signed her teaching certificate that same day.

"How well I remember the preparations," Barton writes in an unpublished manuscript that was intended to follow *The Story of My Childhood*, "the efforts to look larger and older, the examination by the learned committee of one clergyman, one lawyer, and one justice of the peace; the certificate with 'excellent' added at the close."[8]

The assigned school was near the home of Barton's married sister, Sally Vassall, where she arranged to board. Her old fears came out almost immediately, how-

The first school where Barton taught. Barton would teach at many different schools during the next few terms.

ever, when she heard that the last teacher had resigned because the older boys had locked him out of the building for six days in a row. Thus when she arrived at the school on a bright May morning, she was horrified to find no pupils in sight. The door, however, was not locked, and her first day in District 9 was followed by a happy term.

She had her brother David to thank for her strength—she could pitch horseshoes and throw baseballs as well as the boys could. "My school," she said, "was continued beyond the customary length of time, and its only hard feature was our parting."[9] Her school was rated first in discipline, for the new teacher was so well liked and respected that she never had to punish any of her forty students.

Teachers like Barton, who taught only the summer sessions, were not considered master teachers and had to be certified for each term. She was given a different school each of the next several summer terms. Soon she was certified for winter terms as well. She explained in a manuscript, portions of which were later published by William E. Barton, how she happened to go to so many schools:

> [A] few times in those years I was borrowed, for a part of a winter term, by some neighboring town, where it would be said there was trouble, and some school was "not getting on well." I usually found that report to be largely illusive, for they got on very well with me. Probably it was the old adage of a "new broom," for I did nothing but teach them. . . . That early and undeserved reputation for "discipline" always clung to me.[10]

After completing her first six years of teaching, Barton established her own school in North Oxford and taught there for four consecutive years. She lived at home and saved her money. She even earned an extra salary by keeping the financial records of her brothers' businesses. She also followed the advice of a family friend, Senator Alexander DeWitt of Massachusetts, and invested some of her money.

Back to School

In 1849, after nearly ten years of teaching, Clara was still living with her aging parents.

A photo of Barton taken at the time she had established her own school and, for her time, become quite a successful entrepreneur.

Biographer Blanche Colton Williams writes that she was

> a well-balanced, capable woman, nearly twenty-nine years of age. For some time she had been looking about her and taking stock. She felt young, she was young, but many of her older pupils had married, their children now in her schools. "Why, they're already calling me Aunt Clara!" To childhood associates she was, like themselves, an aging woman. More ambitious than her beaux [male friends], more and more out of intellectual harmony with her girl and woman friends, despite affection for them and for her family, she stood alone.[11]

Barton also realized that she was beyond the age at which most women of the time married. According to Williams, she was "suspended between the generations."[12] Perhaps partly for this reason, she decided to enter the Liberal Institute, an advanced school for female teachers in Clinton, New York. In spite of their regrets at losing her bookkeeping services, Stephen and David took their sister to Clinton for the 1850–1851 school year.

At the institute Clara perfected her formal and somewhat flowery style of writing. She took all the education and methods courses the institute offered and even some private studies, particularly French, from professors at nearby Hamilton College.

While Clara was in Clinton, her mother, Sarah Stone Barton, died. Her father went to live with Stephen Jr., relieving her of any concern over his care. The future founder of the American Red Cross was free to pursue her lifework.

No Wedding for Miss Barton

During her teaching years, says Williams,

> Clara felt and behaved as she was—a vigorous New England young woman, active in the present but sure of an expanding future toward which she marched with a romantic eye, alert for what the years would bring.[13]

She enjoyed picking berries and nuts, playing games, and going to parties. But she did not fall in love. There were proposals of marriage from three of many male friends, but none of these offers ended in a wedding. In later years she told her nephew that "not one of the men approached her ideal of a husband."[14]

One suitor was a handsome cousin, another was a fellow boarder in the home of an Oxford family where Barton stayed while she was teaching. She never identified the third man in her writings. She liked and enjoyed all three but found it hard to think of her own happiness while she made up her mind. After much agony of heart, she refused all her suitors, apparently having resolved that in this one instance she would seek her own interests.

In 1849 one of the men who loved her went to California and made a fortune panning gold. But when he came back, he found she was still firm in her decision. This man, whose anonymity has been protected by Barton and all her biographers, insisted on giving her $10,000 (a huge amount of money for the time) as a gift. Although she accepted it, she never spent it on herself. She used the money once and then repaid it to her savings account, where it drew interest and became a legacy in her will.

Private and Public Education in New Jersey

After a year at the Liberal Institute, Barton accepted the invitation of a classmate, Mary Norton, to teach in Hightstown, New Jersey. Barton's reputation for excellent teaching spread in New Jersey as it had in Massachusetts. Soon she heard about the need for a good teacher ten miles away in Bordentown.

The New Jersey schools to which Barton was appointed were private schools. Before long, however, she saw that most of the children in Bordentown were not attending classes. The tuition was too high for some; religious differences kept others away from schools that were founded by one or another church-related group.

By visiting the school superintendent, Barton learned that although New Jersey laws required public schools, the laws were neither respected nor enforced. The school board thought that there was too much division in the population for the public schools to succeed.

Fired by enthusiasm to fill the needs of the children, Barton offered to teach for three months with no pay. All children who came to her classroom would be accepted. This, she said, would prove that the children wanted to learn. Education would be good for them and would benefit the whole town. The school board agreed to find her a building.

Only six students came on the first day, but the next day all of them brought their friends. Before five weeks were up, the number had increased to two hun-

dred, and Barton had to call on a friend from the Liberal Institute to come and help her. By the end of the year the school board had provided a building with eight rooms for the six hundred pupils who wanted to attend the public school.

When the 1853–1854 school year opened, Barton experienced the bitterness of having her career blocked by her gender. The school board thought the work she had been doing was too important for a woman. They did not want to offer a woman the salary that normally would have been paid to the superintendent of such a large school. They appointed J. Kirby Burham as superintendent and paid him twice as much money as Barton had received.

Soon her authority and policies were challenged and changed. By midwinter the effort of trying to support Burham and still work in the school brought on complete physical and emotional exhaustion. When she lost her voice from the stress, she saw the opportunity to resign

The school in Bordentown where Barton offered to teach for free in order to prove that, given the opportunity, the children of the town would pursue their education.

One of Miss Barton's First Students

Author Percy H. Epler tells of visiting a pupil who had been in Barton's first class in District 9, Worcester County, Massachusetts. This account is from The Life of Clara Barton.

"In 1914, I visited one of the forty pupils of this first school of Clara's—Mrs. Shumway Davis, who still lives near the Barton homestead. Mrs. Davis, who is eighty-four, was only nine years younger than her teacher. She recalls how Clara Barton at once won her class by taking them into her confidence and drawing them out. Even in the opening Scripture [Bible reading], in place of the Puritan dictatorial sternness, she broke the pedagogic ice by having the children read in turn. Then she asked them what [Jesus] meant in the verses in the Sermon on the Mount.

Social and friendly, she joined with them in the playground till her athletic prowess amazed the four 'roughies' of the school, who at once gave her their right hand of fellowship. Instead of being locked out as the previous teacher had been, she 'locked' herself 'in' the hearts of every boy and girl. It made not only men and women of them, but more—it made them patriots. 'Their blood crimsoned the hardest fields,' Miss Barton once said, recalling how many of this first class had served their country in time of crisis."

without giving anyone further trouble. Although she wrote home to her brother Stephen for advice, she made up her own mind not to return to North Oxford. She went via Baltimore to Washington, D.C., to regain her health and look for work.

A New Career in the Nation's Capital

Clara lived with her sister Sally, who had moved to Washington, D.C., with her husband. The climate and leisure soon restored the younger woman's health. She enjoyed listening to debates in Congress. She continued her study of French. Putting to practice the political education she had received from her father, she visited her friend and financial adviser from Massachusetts, Senator Alexander DeWitt.

DeWitt advised her to apply for a position in the U.S. Patent Office. Soon she wrote home describing the marble halls of the Patent Office Building and the process of obtaining a patent. She could accurately and neatly copy ten thousand

Washington, D.C., in 1853, where Barton went to start anew.

A session of Congress at the time Barton was living in Washington, D.C. She enjoyed attending congressional debates.

words a day in a clear, regular, easy-to-read script. For at least her first year she copied documents and was paid by the page. Barton's speed and accuracy were rewarded when she obtained a position as temporary clerk. She held this position in the all-male bureaucracy until 1857. She claims that she was the first woman to draw a salary from the government in her own name. Objections to a woman patent office employee interrupted Barton's work, however. Her job was eliminated, and she returned to North Oxford.

Barton had thought that her dismissal from the patent office would bring her Washington, D.C., life to a close. But a couple of years later she was called back.

The Decision Not to Marry

Between April 20 and May 25, 1852, says biographer William E. Barton, his cousin solved her love problem. During an interview with one of her friends, he received this analysis of Clara's decision.

"For ten years after she began to teach, she was shut out from any real opportunity for love. Her elevation to the teacher's platform, while still a child, shut out her normal opportunity for innocent flirtation. Love hardly peeped in at her during her teens, or in her early twenties. By the time it came to her, other interests had gained a long start. She was ambitious, she was determined to find out what she was good for, and to do something worth while in life. Had some young man come into her life as worthy as those who made love to her, and who was her equal or superior in ability and education, she might have learned to love him. As it was, she decided wisely both for herself and for the men who sought her hand.

Having thus chosen, she did not mourn her fate. She enjoyed friendships with men and with women, and lived her busy, successful, and happy life. She did not talk of these affairs, nor did she write of them. . . .

From one who knew her intimately in those days, I have this statement:

'Clara Barton had many admirers, and they were all men whom she admired and some whom she almost loved. More men were interested in her than she was ever interested in; some of them certainly interested her, yet not profoundly. I do not think she ever had a love affair that stirred the depths of her being. The truth is, Clara Barton was herself so much stronger a character than any of the men who made love to her that I do not think she was ever seriously tempted to marry any of them. She was so pronounced in her opinions that a man who wanted a submissive wife would have stood somewhat in awe of her. However good a wife she might have made to a man whom she knew to be her equal, and for whom she felt real admiration, she would not have been an ideal wife for a man . . . whom she could not look up [to,] not only in regard to moral character, which in every case was above reproach, but also as to intellect, education, and ambition.'"

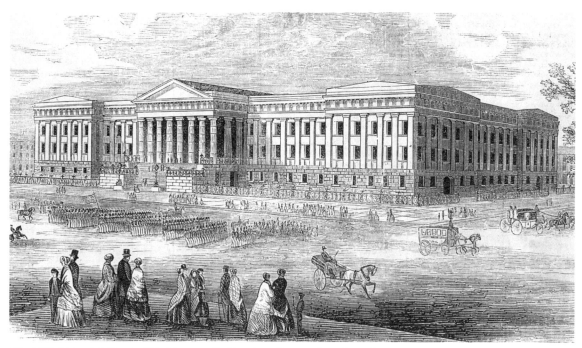

The U.S. Patent Office in Washington, D.C., where Barton found employment as a clerk. She was the only woman working at the patent office.

By the latter part of 1860 the integrity of the patent office was threatened. Dishonest clerks were secretly copying confidential documents that passed through the office and selling them for their own profit. The superintendent of patents, Charles Mason, asked Barton to help him reestablish the confidentiality of the patent process. She believed in the importance of her work, which, she said in a letter to a friend, was

> a record which must live and be legible when the mound which once covered me shall have become a hollow and the moss-covered headstone with "born" and "died" no longer to be traced upon its time-worn front shall have buried itself beneath the kindred turf.[15]

Chapter

3 Behind the Lines in the American Civil War

Barton had returned to the U.S. Patent Office just before seven states seceded from the Union and formed the Confederate States of America. Barton avidly followed the passionate congressional debates that followed secession. When Senator Charles Sumner of Massachusetts was assaulted following his speech against slavery, Barton was in the visitors' gallery. Her letters of those months of the debate on slavery in the new territory of Kansas show her emotional involvement with every stage in the conflict between the North and the South.

Despite months of Confederate threats over the Union army's occupation of Fort Sumter in South Carolina, the North was not prepared for the actual outbreak of war. Lincoln had arrived in Washington only nine days before his inauguration. He had barely appointed his cabinet when Confederate troops fired on Fort Sumter on April 12, 1861, and four more states, including Virginia, joined the Confederacy. Knowing that Washington, D.C., now on the border of a hostile state, was also a possible target for attack, President Lincoln called for a volunteer army to defend the nation's capital.

Among the Massachusetts volunteer regiments traveling south through New

The Confederate army fires on Fort Sumter in South Carolina in 1861. The attack signaled the beginning of the Civil War.

Men from the Massachusetts volunteer regiments are attacked by mobs favoring the cause of the South. When the wounded volunteers arrived in Washington, Barton set to work caring for them.

York and Maryland were men who had been Barton's pupils in Worcester County. In Baltimore, only forty miles from Confederate territory, the men were attacked and plundered by mobs who favored the cause of the South. Arriving in Washington, wounded and without their baggage, the soldiers found no place to stay, not even tents. Finally, the unprepared War Department assigned them quarters in the Senate building. On a warm day, April 25, 1861, Clara Barton observed in a letter:

> The city is filling up with troops. The Massachusetts regiment is quartered in the Capitol and the 7th arrived today at noon. Almost a week in getting from New York here; they looked tired and worn, but sturdy and brave. . . . We visited the regiment yesterday at the Capitol; found some old friends and acquaintances from Worcester; their baggage was all seized and they have *nothing* but their heavy woolen clothes—not a cotton shirt—and many of them not even a pocket handkerchief. We, of course, emptied our pockets and came home to tear up old sheets for towels and handkerchiefs, and have filled a large box with all manner of serving utensils, thread, needles, thimbles, scissors, pins, buttons, strings, salves, tallow, etc., etc., have filled the largest market basket in the house and it will go to them in the next hour.[16]

Along with the basket of supplies collected for the soldiers in the Senate building, Barton brought a copy of the hometown newspaper, the *Worcester Spy*. From a perch on the desk of the president of the Senate, she read the entire paper to the Massachusetts troops.

Reading that paper and knowing about military authority, Barton saw a quick way to get help from the soldiers' relatives and friends. The following week, the *Spy* published her advertisement to the people of Worcester County to send food and clothing, or money for her to buy things their sons and brothers needed. So many boxes were delivered that she hardly had room to sort their contents.

The War Gets Off to a Slow Start

Although the Confederate army did not attack the District of Columbia, the whole area was affected by the threat of military action. The volunteer Union army set up tents in the hills surrounding the city awaiting their orders. Barton scouted around among the seventy-five thousand homesick soldiers, looking for men from Massachusetts to receive the supplies that had been sent. One of Barton's biographers, Ishbel Ross, writes:

> From small beginnings her work spread out in all directions. She wrote letters for the soldiers. She notified their mothers of their condition. In turn, comforts were sent to her, and families inquired about their boys. Her needs were lavishly advertised by word of mouth in New England. Churches, sewing circles, and relief committees responded with enthusiasm.[17]

The soldiers finally set off on their hundred-mile march south to attack the new Confederate capital, Richmond, Virginia, and to win the Confederate States back for the Union. For four days a continuous column marched out of Washington, as Barton wrote to her father, "noble, gallant, handsome fellows, armed to the teeth, apparently lacking nothing."[18] Followed by a merry crowd of sightseers who wanted to view a war, they had gone about thirty miles when the Confederate army met them at the little north-flowing river called Bull Run, on July 21, 1861. Here the Union army was ruinously defeated

The Battle of Bull Run ended with a Union defeat and nearly three thousand men dead. The defeat brought home the seriousness of the newly begun war.

and lost 2,952 men. Now the truth of the war came home. A shattered army streamed back into the capital. A thousand wounded men flooded the hospitals.

Gathering Supplies

Barton went to the hospitals to help, but as battle after battle was fought, the stories told of suffering at the line of battle showed her a greater need. One story after another reflected the terrible scarcity of supplies and lack of care. As winter set in, wounded soldiers died of exposure. Many could have been saved if there had been supplies and nurses on the spot. Each regiment furnished its own uniforms, and some were inadequate. Barton advertised for supplies and built up her stores to send to the front—bandages, jellies, socks, gloves. Each army continued to fight to extend its borders.

As news came back, Barton wanted to help at the front. She wrote of her ideas on how to supply the emergency needs of fighting men in a letter to the secretary of the Ladies Relief Committee of Worcester, Massachusetts:

> I will not hesitate to advance [this idea] on my own responsibility, [namely], that every State should have . . . a depot of her own where all her contributions should be sent and dispersed; if her own soldiers need it all, to them; if not, then let her share generously and intelligently with those who do need; but know what she has and what she gives. . . . When the storehouse of any State should be found empty, it would be safe to conclude that her troops are in need; then let the full garners

[storehouses] render the required assistance. This would systematize the whole matter and do away with all unnecessary confusion, doubt, and uncertainty.[19]

Clearly there was a need for organization, as every day brought new stories of hardship. Barton saw more and more clearly that the mode of delivery service to the battlefield itself needed to be changed.

Courage After Visiting Her Soldier Father

Barton's work and plans were interrupted at the beginning of February 1862, with news of her father's illness. She went to North Oxford to be with him, and to share her misgivings about the efficiency of the War Department's Sanitary Commission, whose job it was to take care of the wounded and slain. She asked his opinion about her growing desire to be of greater assistance. His assurance that her presence would be respected and appreciated strengthened her determination to go to the front.

She wrote of her father's failing condition to her brother Stephen, who had moved his sawmill and lumber business to Hertford County, North Carolina, now behind the enemy lines. She begged him to join her, to trust that his property would be protected, but he chose not to leave North Carolina. Stephen's decision caused his sister much worry as the war went on and eventually resulted in his capture and imprisonment.

Although women were not allowed on the field, nor wanted there by the army au-

Volunteers Assisting the wounded on the field of Battle

(Left) Volunteers assist the wounded in the field of battle. Barton was frustrated by the inefficiency of government efforts to care for sick and wounded soldiers. Hearing the news that the Union army of Gen. George McClellan (pictured below) was doing poorly in battle, Barton's decision to help the wounded gained new urgency.

thorities, Barton relied on her father's encouragement. Fired with patriotism and grieved over the downturn of Gen. George Brinton McClellan's campaign to take Richmond, she schemed and wrote letters for passes to the battlefield. And while she waited for the needed military approval, she set up central collection places to ensure a constant flow of food, medicines, bandages, clothing, and bedding.

Military Passes to the Front

More than three months elapsed before Barton's patience with military protocol was rewarded. On July 11, 1862, William A. Hammond, the U.S. surgeon general, granted her permission to "transport comforts to the wounded and sick . . . subject

The passes Barton received to carry supplies and aid the wounded on the front lines. After acquiring the required passes, Barton made her first expedition on August 3, 1862.

always to the direction of the surgeon in charge."[20] Within the next month Clara had secured the required passes for her trip to the front. Driving a wagon loaded with supplies, she began her first personal expedition on Sunday, August 3, 1862. Her destination was Fredericksburg, Virginia. She delivered her stores, waited during the night, then went to visit the hospital at Fredericksburg and the camp of the 21st Massachusetts Regiment. By

6:00 P.M. on August 5, she was back in Washington, with new ideas.

Another Barton biographer, Percy H. Epler, notes that at this time both the Sanitary Commission and its volunteer partner, the Christian Commission, operated entirely behind the lines: "Not only had no woman gone to the firing line, but it was before organized aid had come to the relief of the soldier, before the two great and noble commissions, with which she was never connected, had found their way directly to the front."[21]

News of the slaughter at Culpeper, Virginia, on August 9, 1862, firmed Barton's purpose. On August 11, she was at Cedar Mountain, where 314 were killed, 1,465 wounded, and 622 reported missing in action from the Union forces. The Confederate army casualties from a force of 20,000 totaled 241 killed, 1,130 wounded, and 1,365 missing or captured. Soldiers from both sides received her impartial attention.

In the Heat of Battle

The casualty figures—thousands killed and wounded—continued to mount. The nation learned of 7,000 wounded at Groveton, Virginia. At Manassas and the Second Battle of Bull Run in Virginia, 800 were killed, 4,000 wounded, and 3,000 captured or missing.

In the Battle of Chantilly in Virginia, Barton wrapped up the mangled arm of Charley Hamilton, one of her first pupils in District 9. She rested briefly while she sat with a crying soldier. She built fires in the rain, cooked meals for hundreds, and used her last bit of food. In her diary she wrote:

In the midst of all this [rain] . . . nearly alone, for my worn-out assistants could work no longer, I continued to administer such food as I had left.

Do you begin to wonder what it could be? Army crackers put into knapsacks and haversacks and beaten to crumbs between stones, and stirred into a mixture of wine, whiskey and water, and sweetened with coarse brown sugar.

Not very inviting you will think but I assure it was always acceptable.[22]

Taking little rest from several days of caring for the wounded at Chantilly, Barton returned to Washington long enough to resupply her wagon before starting to Alexandria. Many years later, she reviewed the experience in a letter to a friend:

We knew this was the last. We put the thousand wounded men we then had into the train. I took one carload of them and Mrs. M. another. The men took to the horses. We steamed off and two hours later there was no Fairfax Station. We reached Alexandria at 10 o'clock at night, and oh, the repast which met those poor men at the train. The people . . . are the most noble I ever saw or heard of. I stood in my car and fed the men till they could eat no more. Then the people would

Before Barton became involved, organizations that cared for the wounded, such as the Christian Commission, worked far behind the battle lines.

A Rain-Soaked Rest

Clara Barton served at the Battle of Chantilly, August 31, 1862. In a letter that appears in The Life of Clara Barton *by Percy H. Epler, she writes how she finally found a few moments to sleep after the train left Chantilly with the wounded.*

"The departure of this train cleared the grounds of wounded for the night, and as the line of fire from its plunging engines died out in the darkness, a strange sensation of weakness and weariness fell upon me, almost defying my utmost exertion to move one foot before the other.

A little Sibley tent had been hastily pitched for me in a slight hollow upon the hillside. Your imaginations will not fail to picture its condition. Rivulets of water had rushed through it during the last three hours. Still I attempted to reach it, as its white surface, in the darkness, was a protection from the wheels of wagons and trampling of beasts.

Perhaps I shall never forget the painful effort which the making of those few rods [probably less than fifty yards], and the gaining of the tent cost me. How many times I fell from sheer exhaustion, in the darkness and mud of that slippery hillside, I have no knowledge, but at last I grasped the welcome canvas, and a well established brook which washing in on the upper side at the opening that served as door, met me on my entrance. My entire floor was covered with water, not an inch of dry, solid ground. . . .

I remember myself sitting on the ground, upheld by my left arm, my head resting on my hand, impelled by an almost uncontrollable desire to lie completely down, and prevented by the certain conviction that if I did, water would flow into my ears.

How long I balanced between my desires and cautions, I have no positive knowledge, but it is very certain that the former carried the point by the position from which I was aroused at twelve o'clock by the rumbling of more wagons of wounded men. I slept two hours, and oh, what strength I had gained! I may never know two other hours of equal worth. I sprang to my feet dripping wet, covered with ridges of dead grass and leaves, wrung the water from my hair and skirts, and went forth again to my work."

An idealized painting depicts Barton aiding the wounded. Barton's brave sallies to the front lines helped win her respect and admiration.

take us home and feed us, and after that we came home. I had slept one and one-half hours since Saturday night and I am well and strong and wait to go again if I have need.[23]

On the battlefield, Barton's strength seemed inexhaustible. When others were in need, she was fearless. When she returned from the Second Battle of Bull Run, which the Union also lost, she wrote of the ordeal, "You have the full record of my sleep—from Friday night till Wednesday morning—two hours. You will not wonder that I slept during the next twenty-four."[24]

Brief Respite, Then Back Again

While at Antietam, Maryland, scene of one of the war's bloodiest battles, Barton came down with a fever and was taken back to Washington. After barely six weeks of rest, she returned to the front. The winter campaign for Fredericksburg surpassed the horrors of what had gone before. It culminated in a fierce battle on December 13, 1862. The Confederate army held the heights of Fredericksburg and stationed snipers in the cellars. Barton watched artillery slaughter the Union forces as they built a rope and pontoon bridge across the Rappahannock River. She wrote:

> It were long to tell of that night crossing and the next terrible day of fire and blood. And when the battle broke o'er field and grove, like a resistless flood daylight exposed Fredericksburg with its fourth-day flag of truce, its dead, starving and wounded frozen to the ground. The wounded were brought to me frozen, for days after, and our commissions and supplies [were in] Washington with no effective organization or power to go beyond. The many wounded lay, uncared for, on the cold snow.[25]

When the army surgeon called for help, Barton crossed the pontoon bridge under fire. Despite a disabling infection in her hand and completely inadequate facilities, she kept on. Her diary contains this description:

> Twelve hundred men were crowded into the Lacy House, which contained but twelve rooms. They covered every foot of the floors and porticos and even lay on the stair landings! A man who could find opportunity to lie between the legs of a table thought himself lucky. He was not like to be stepped on. In a common cupboard, with four shelves, five men lay, and were fed and attended. Three lived to be removed, and two died of their wounds.[26]

And the men were grateful. Many of them survived. When Barton returned to Washington in the spring of 1863, she was called to Ward 17 of Lincoln Hospital. Seventy men saluted her,

standing such as could, others rising feebly in their beds, and falling back—exhausted with the effort.

Every man had left his blood in Fredericksburg—every one was from Lacy House. My hand had dressed every wound—many of them in the first terrible moments of agony. I had prepared their food in the snow and winds of December and fed them like children.[27]

Barton Moves South and Becomes Superintendent of Nurses

The war was to continue for another two years. In the west the Union's Vicksburg campaign succeeded in July 1863, cutting off the Confederate food supply by gaining control of the Mississippi River. General Robert E. Lee's Gettysburg campaign to invade Pennsylvania and Maryland from the south was stopped.

After the navy moved into Charleston Bay, South Carolina, to retake Fort Sumter, Barton served there for eight months, beginning April 7, 1863. She lived on Hilton Head in a hospital tent. Here the relative routine of hospital service and cooking for the wounded allowed her an occasional horseback ride with an officer, a brief visit with her brother David at the quartermaster tent, or a word with his fourteen-year-old son, Stephen, in the Military Telegraph Department.

In May 1864 Barton accepted an appointment in a Union unit as superintendent of nurses. Behind the firing line ten miles from Fredericksburg, during the series of engagements known as the Battle of Spotsylvania, May 8–12, 1864, she came upon stalled wagons of wounded men. Riding farther, she found they were stuck in knee-deep mud from the spring rains. Moreover, certain officers were refusing to order the people of Fredericksburg to open their homes to the wounded.

Helpless to override these officers' authority, Barton went to their superiors. In a matter-of-fact manner her diary recounts a truly remarkable accomplishment:

> With difficulty I obtained . . . four stout horses with a light army wagon [that] took me ten miles at an unbroken gallop, through field and swamp, and stumps and mud to Belle Plain and a steam tug at once to Washington. Landing at dusk I sent for Henry Wilson, Chairman of the Military Committee of the Senate. A messenger brought him at eight, saddened and appalled like every other patriot in that fearful hour, at the weight of woe under which the nation staggered, groaned, and wept. . . . Both railroad and canal were opened. In three days I returned with carloads of supplies.[28]

Because the Civil War was a war of attrition, generals sought to kill more soldiers than the enemy. This tactic resulted in astronomical casualty rates. Here, surgeons—in the midst of battle—operate on a wounded soldier.

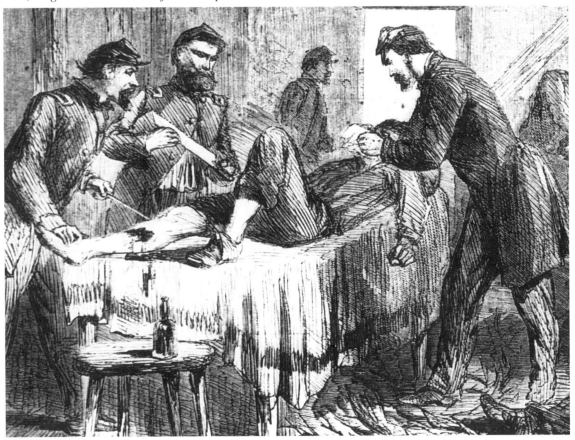

Barton Grieves over the Loss of Life

As the victories and defeats were tallied, Barton reflected on the terrible losses the country had sustained. This comment is from one of her diaries, included in the biography by Percy H. Epler.

"Victory, yes! but oh, the cost! The desolation, the woe, and the want, that spread over the whole land. 13,000 dead in one prison! 300,000 dead in one year! Dead everywhere! On every battle field they lie! In the crowded yards of every prison ground! In the dark ravines of the tangled forest! In the miry prison swamps, where the slimy serpent crawls by day, and the will-o'-the-wisp dances at night! In the beds of the mighty rivers! Under the waves of the salt sea! In the drifting sands of the desert islands! On the lonely picket line! And by the roadside, where the weary soldier lay down with his knapsack, and his gun, and his march of life was ended! There in the strange beds they sleep, till the morning of the great reveille!

Facing the frowning battlements of Petersburg, Richmond and Charleston, and the flower of the Rebel Army, there I saw them fight and die. And there, with their Eastern comrades, their bones whiten in the sand. The fields of Virginia are rich with their blood."

A Civil War soldier lies dead behind a defensive battlement. Barton was dismayed by the sheer number of dead and wounded the war produced.

Clara's Brother a Prisoner of War

Barton joined Gen. Benjamin Franklin Butler's army in the siege of Petersburg, which lasted from June 5, 1864, to April 1, 1865.

That winter Butler's men picked up Barton's brother Stephen. They had come across him, forty miles from his North Carolina home, hoping to buy medicine to relieve the severe congestion in his lungs. Supposing him to be a southern sympathizer, they seized his money and took him to the Norfolk prison camp.

When Barton heard the news, she went directly to Butler to assure him that Stephen was loyal to the Union and to ask for his release. The general had him brought to camp, malnourished and feverish. Soon cleared of charges, he shared the little slave cabin where his sister slept. She cared for his needs in between preparing special pies and custards, superintending the camp cooking, and riding once a week to the base hospital for supplies.

The Sanitary Commission had become better organized to care for the soldiers' needs, and the army was not on the field, so Barton also had time to write many letters, probably sitting at the pine writing desk her brother David had constructed for her. As would be seen before the end of the decade, one letter made an important contact with the sister of a Swiss volunteer, Jules Golay.

Stephen's health did not improve, and he was moved to Washington, where Barton visited him as often as she could. Stephen died on March 10, 1865, and was buried in the home plot at Worcester, Massachusetts.

Stephen Barton's experiences as a prisoner of war and his prayers for peace had a lasting effect on his sister Clara. She took up the letter-writing campaign that would become her postwar work, that of finding soldiers reported missing in action.

4 Missing Soldiers and a National Memorial

Reading the accumulation of mail that she found whenever she returned to her apartment in Washington, Barton began to realize how many men were unaccounted for. Many of the letters carried words of thanks for her service at the front, but more pleaded for information about sons, brothers, and fathers who had not been heard from.

Barton had often filled her pockets with notes to help in contacting people, and her memory contained many other details. She had sent many a dying soldier's message to a friend or relative. Probably no woman in the United States had seen so much blood and suffering as she had during her three years on the battlefield. As on the battlefield, she took her motto seriously: "You must never think of anything except the need, and how to meet it."[29]

In January 1865 she asked her sister Sally Vassall to help her answer the mail. In February, with a few friends in Annapolis, Maryland, Barton privately established the Office of Correspondence with Friends of the Missing Men of the United States Army.

Finding all these missing men was not a task for a private individual. Barton needed governmental authority to examine military records. She needed to check

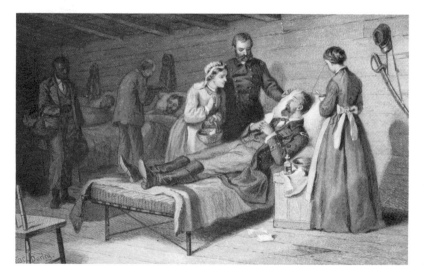

A dying soldier writes his last letter home. Barton was instrumental in organizing volunteers to help answer letters from family members asking about missing soldiers.

Secretary of War Edwin Stanton had final approval of Barton's request to aid in the search for missing soldiers. She was never able to contact him directly.

names in letters from relatives against official lists of the dead and wounded. She needed money for postage, secretarial help, and record keeping. Since the nation was still at war, Secretary of War Stanton would have to approve any idea involving the military. Full clearance, a budget, and a government position were essential to the success of her project to locate missing soldiers.

In her best script, she wrote a petition to the president and went to the White House to deliver it and speak with him:

> To His Excellency
> Abraham Lincoln
> President of the United States
> Sir:
> I most respectfully solicit your authority and endorsement to allow me to act temporarily as General Correspondent at Annapolis, Maryland, hav-

ing in view the reception and answering of letters from the friends of our prisoners now being exchanged.

It will be my object also to obtain and furnish all possible information in regard to those that have died during their confinement.

Hoping that the objects contemplated may commend themselves to your favorable consideration.

Yours Most respectfully,
Clara Barton.[30]

Senator Henry Wilson, still serving on the Committee of Military Affairs, happened along as Barton was leaving the White House one day, disappointed over failing to gain admittance to Lincoln's

When Barton failed to gain access to Lincoln to discuss her plan, Senator Henry Wilson offered to take up her cause with the president.

A Letter About a Missing Brother

Barton's interest in each person shows in this letter to Postmaster Alexander in Washington. Alexander had received a request from the sister of Thomas Luthers, who had run away before he was fourteen and enlisted in the Union army in Chester County, Pennsylvania. The letter, written early in 1869, appears in Daughter of Destiny.

"Dear Sir:

Your kind letter enclosing that of Mrs. Reighner, concerning the little drummer boy is received. It will be exceedingly difficult to get any trace of him unless some information can be gathered of the regiment he enlisted in. I will wait a few days in the hope that some clue may be given you by the sister; if not the best method will be to apply to the Adjt. [Adjutant] General of the State of Pennsylvania, and by causing close search among the records of Chester County. They will find him unless (as is very probably) he assumed [another] name, in which case all is lost. His tiny bones rest and whiten with the great unknown army of sleeping martyrs bivouacked from the Susquehanna [River] to the Rio Grande and the name his mother called him by, and his dark little history stand on the pages of the Recording Angel, if the pitying tear did not blot them out.

Nothing in the whole war so tried my soul as the sight of the poor little shelterless fellows, scarce better than babies, drumming their way to eternity.

If nothing is heard which can assist the search in a few days, if you will address the [Adjutant] Genl's office of this city, I will [address] that in Pennsylvania and see what comes of our inquiry. Possibly they will give us closer attention than they would the sister.

With very great respect,
I am most truly yours
Clara Barton."

office. Wilson offered to take the petition to the president. Again, Barton waited, but there was no word from the president. She spoke to the head of volunteers, Gen. E. A. Hitchcock, who thought her plan a good one. So, too, did Gen. W. Hoffman, commissioner general of prisoners. These influential men advised her to go ahead with her office of correspondence but could not give her governmental permission. In her diary, she wrote:

I dare not [go ahead]. I do not feel it my duty to bring myself to public mortification in order to do a public charity. I am certain that if I publish my intention Secretary Stanton will follow it with a card to the effect that I am acting without authority.[31]

Lincoln's reelection in 1864 and the inaugural ball that followed on March 4, 1865, offered Barton another chance to meet with the president. Dressed in a new green silk dress, Barton hoped for a moment with the president. That moment never came. Frustrated and disappointed, she was back in the White House the next day and the next, hoping for a few minutes of his time. Finally, on March 11, 1865, Clara received a copy of the following letter:

To the Friends of Missing Persons.

Miss Clara Barton has kindly offered to search for the missing prisoners of war. Please address her in Annapolis, giving her name, regiment, and company of any missing prisoner.

[Signed] A. Lincoln[32]

More Setbacks

Barton took heart from Lincoln's letter. Peace seemed near. Richmond surrendered on April 3, 1865, the Confederacy collapsed, and General Lee surrendered at Appomattox Courthouse April 9. But five days later, President Lincoln was fatally shot. Filled with grief and apprehension, Barton worried over her newest project and the fate of the country under Andrew Johnson, the new president. One bound collection of letters shows that while Lincoln's body lay in state in the Capitol, Barton answered a hundred inquiries about missing men.

With the letter from Lincoln, Barton convinced the War Department to give her a little office in Annapolis. Department authorities let her look through some information about missing prisoners, but not nearly enough to fulfill the many requests. Many soldiers had been buried in unmarked graves on prison grounds and on the battlefield. Of the Union dead, more than 172,000 were

Gen. Robert E. Lee surrenders to General Grant at Appomattox Courthouse.

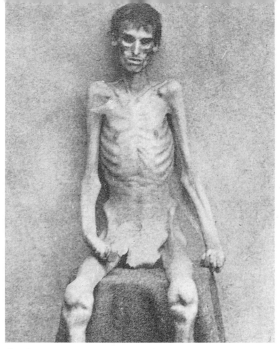

Little more than a gaunt skeleton, this starving prisoner is graphic testimony to the atrocities of Andersonville and other prison camps.

identified at the end of the war. But Union officials had counted twice as many graves. An additional 44,000 listed dead were without known grave sites, for a total of nearly 360,000 deaths, less than half of whom were named.

There was ample evidence that many people did not know the fate of their relatives and friends. Letters told of soldiers who had lost all track of their families and did not know what had happened to them or where to write. The newspapers seemed the logical way to bring the information together. Epler writes that

> May 15, 1865, found a mass of unanswered letters in her hands with new ones coming in at the rate of 100 per day. Miss Barton's strategic and never-losing stroke was now an appeal to the country. This plea to the people, like every other she made, was eminently

successful. The country responded to her requests for information with a pathetic eagerness. All types and conditions of [people] sent information to her.[33]

The information received went far beyond what could be written in individual letters by a few faithful people. Lists of names would have to be printed and sent all over the country so that everyone who might possibly recognize a name could read the lists and provide clues to the identities of the missing men.

The cost of reproducing thousands of lists was also looming as a serious problem. Barton had been buying the stamps for her many letters, but printing the lists of names and mailing them to newspapers and courthouses around the country was more than she could do on her limited funds. She borrowed from her savings account the entire precious $10,000 gift of her rejected suitor, along with the $5,000 interest it had by this time earned. But even that was not enough. She advertised for donations to help with the publication of twenty thousand copies of the lists.

Clara and her sister Sally, with three helpers, Edward Shaw, Samuel Ramsey, and the Swiss volunteer Jules Golay, copied names from the letters and from the rolls of missing men and looked for a printer to publish the lists. In those precomputer days, when copy to be printed was composed one letter at a time from sets of metal type, the only printer with enough capital letters to do the job was the Government Printing Office, which finally received authorization for the work.

The publication of Barton's lists brought her work to the attention of Dorence Atwater, a former Union soldier who had been a prisoner of war in Andersonville, Georgia. While in prison he had worked as a clerk, listing the names of the prisoners who had died. Deaths from dysentery, gangrene, and starvation had occurred at the rate of more than a hundred a day. In seven months, more than ten thousand died in the Andersonville prison.

Millen Prison's Missing Soldiers

Former Confederate prisoner John McElroy, who was detained at Millen Prison, in eastern Georgia, wrote about his experiences for an Ohio newspaper. Later the articles were expanded into a book incorporating the stories of other prison survivors as well. The book, This Was Andersonville, *suggests how it happened that many men died and were buried without anyone recording these events.*

"The lagging leaden hours were inexpressibly dreary. Compared with many others, we were quite comfortable, as our hut protected us from the actual beating of the rain upon our bodies. But we were much more miserable than under the sweltering heat of Andersonville as we lay almost naked upon our bed of pine leaves, shivering in the raw rasping air, and looked out over acres of wretches lying dumbly on the sodden sand, receiving the benumbing drench of the sullen skies without a groan or a motion.

It was enough to kill healthy vigorous men, active and resolute, with bodies well-nourished and well-clothed and with minds vivacious and hopeful, to stand these days-and-night-long cold drenchings. No one can imagine how fatal it was to boys whose vitality was sapped by long months in Andersonville, by the coarse, meager, changeless food, by the grovelling on the bare earth, and by the hopelessness as to any improvement of conditions. Fever, rheumatism, throat and lung diseases and despair now came to complete the work begun by scurvy, dysentery and gangrene in Andersonville. Hundreds, weary of the long struggle and, hoping against hope, laid themselves down and yielded to their fate. In the six weeks that we were at Millen, one man in every ten died. The ghostly pines there sigh over the unnoted graves of seven hundred boys for whom life's morning closed in the gloomiest shadows. As many as would form a splendid regiment, as many as constitute the first-born of a city populace, more than three times as many as were slain outright on our side in the bloody battle of Franklin [Tennessee, in 1864] succumbed to this new hardship. The country for which they died does not even have record of their names."

With the help of notes taken by an ex-prisoner, Barton was able to help identify Union soldiers who were listed as missing, but who had died and been buried at Andersonville.

Atwater wrote down the name, home state, date, cause of death, company, and regiment of each soldier who died at Andersonville. Horrified by the terrible conditions in the prison and the disorganized approach to keeping records of the dead, Atwater realized that his work for the prison authorities would almost certainly be lost or destroyed. So he secretly made a duplicate list and sewed it into the lining of his coat. By the time he was moved to another prison in February 1865, he had preserved the record of about thirteen thousand men who were buried at Andersonville.

Atwater eventually offered his list to the War Department, but no one took any action. So he told Clara Barton his story. She immediately recognized that these names, written in order of their places of burial, could be matched with the lists she had made from the letters of inquiry she had received.

With her brother Stephen's experience as a prisoner of war still fresh in her memory, she presented a plan to General Hoffman. They would go to Andersonville to mark the graves and enclose the burial grounds so that they could be visited by the bereaved families. Secretary of War Stanton agreed to her plan for the cemetery and appointed Capt. James M. Moore, assistant quartermaster, to head an expedition to Andersonville. Taking Barton and Atwater with him on July 8, 1865, Moore sailed south, then continued west by railroad, with grave markers, fencing, paint, nails, and a crew of workmen. They identified and marked 12,920 graves on the nine-acre grounds and built gates and walks.

On August 17 Barton commemorated the finding of nearly thirteen thousand men by raising the flag for the Andersonville Cemetery dedication ceremony.

She also recorded the evidence that remained of the wretched conditions in which the prisoners of war had lived. In the report she made for Stanton, Barton described wells dug by prisoners in their desperate search for water. She told of soldiers who died when their escape tunnels collapsed. She listed belongings left behind by prisoners—horns used as drinking cups, gourds scooped out and used as bowls and cups, spoons and platters cut out of old canteens, pans and kettles soldered together from pieces of tin or iron.

The Correspondence Office Runs into Difficulty

Upon her return to Washington, Barton found that her funding had fallen victim

W. T. Sherman Views Millen Prison

Gen. William Tecumseh Sherman's diary contains this account of his view of Millen Prison, which he saw during his famous march to the sea. Accounts such as this one, which appears in Sherman's March, *edited by Richard Wheeler, added strength to arguments for more humanitarian treatment of prisoners of war.*

"On the 3d of December I entered Millen [some seventy miles northwest of Savannah] with the Seventeenth Corps . . . and there paused one day to communicate with all parts of the army. . . . The whole army was in good position and in good condition. We had largely subsisted on the country; our wagons were full of forage and provisions; but as we approached the seacoast the country became more sandy and barren, and food became more scarce. Still, with little or no loss we had traveled two-thirds of our distance, and I concluded to push on for Savannah. . . . [First] I caused the fine depot at Millen to be destroyed, and other damage to be done. . . .

[Nearby] . . . was the hideous prison-pen [now empty] used by the enemy for the confinement of Federal [Union] soldiers who had become prisoners of war. A space of ground about three hundred feet square, inclosed by a stockade, without any covering whatsoever, was the hole where thousands of our brave soldiers have been confined for months past, exposed to heavy dews, biting frosts, and pelting rains, without so much as a board or tent to protect them after the Rebels had stolen their clothing. Some of them had adopted the wretched alternative of digging holes in the ground, into which they crept at times. What wonder that we found the evidence that seven hundred and fifty men had died there!"

Sherman's march to the sea. Jubilant freed slaves follow Sherman and his troops. Sherman viewed Millen Prison during this famous march.

to politics and red tape. She searched for a way to give the public a list of the names of the buried prisoners. She again enlisted Atwater's help, this time with a plan to publish the rolls of the Andersonville dead. They persuaded Horace Greeley, editor of the *New York Tribune,* to publish a story about Atwater, as well as an eighty-page pamphlet containing the names from his list of Andersonville dead. The pamphlet sold at newsstands for a quarter.

The publication of the Andersonville lists brought more mail. Letters arrived thanking Barton for relieving people's minds about their missing friends and relatives. But more mail meant the need for more money, and she had depleted her funds by publishing the first series of lists. Not until 1866 did the Senate appropriate $15,000 to repay Barton for her past work. The money, which went back into her savings account to satisfy the loan Barton had made to herself, remained in that account until her death.

A New Opportunity

Publicity now followed Clara Barton wherever she went. Over and above the demand for information about the war were requests for personal appearances and lectures. Barton saw that she could supplement her funds with the small stipends and admission fees that would come from giving talks about her work and experiences.

From 1866 to 1868 Barton gave three hundred lectures on her war experiences. Her audiences included patients and colleagues from the war, their parents, brothers, sisters, cousins, friends, and children.

A flyer would be posted announcing that Miss Barton would be speaking for a twenty-five-cent admission fee. The halls would be crowded. The next day, the newspapers would report a successful speech "that transported the imagination of the hearer to the scenes she so vividly described."[34] Many of Barton's written descriptions of Civil War scenes have come from her talks, some of which were given more than once, as she had limited time to write.

The grueling schedule she worked out for herself included many nighttime trips. She would travel to the lecture site after work at the Office of Correspondence, give her talk, return on the night train or coach, and be at work the next day. Instead of buying a nourishing supper, she would spend the proceeds of her talk on stationery and postage.

Helping the Campaign for Women's Right to Vote

The demands on Barton's time and energy expanded with her popularity. She continued her work on the lists of missing men, and also squeezed in some time for the suffragists, who were agitating for women's suffrage, or the right to vote. Barton was in demand as a speaker at their meetings because men attended her lectures, whereas mostly women came to hear the suffragists.

The well-known reformer Susan B. Anthony invited Barton to the New York meeting of the American Equal Rights Association. After this Barton kept up a connection with equal rights advocates. She became a personal friend of Anthony and

Susan B. Anthony invited Barton to take part in the equal rights movement for women. The two women became close friends.

Another Period of Exhaustion

Barton's accounting in 1869 showed that she had spent $16,759, and distributed 99,057 printed lists and 58,759 flyers. She had supervised 41,855 letters to individuals and 63,182 transfers of information. In the end, notes Ross, "she was responsible for more than 20,000 soldiers being entered on the rolls who otherwise might never have been identified."[36]

Barton maintained her correspondence and lecture circuit without sufficient rest, food, or warmth for nearly three years. This superhuman effort finally caused a physical breakdown even worse than the loss of her voice at the end of her New Jersey public school teaching. Her diary records how her energy failed in Portland, Maine:

One early winter evening in [1868], I stood on the platform of one of the finest new opera houses in the East, filled to repletion with, it seemed to me, the most charming attendance I had ever beheld, plumed and jeweled ladies, stalwart youths, reverend white-haired men, and gradually to my horror I felt my voice giving out, leaving me. The next moment I opened my mouth but no sound followed. Again and again I attempted it, with no result. It was finished! Nervous prostration had declared itself. I went to my home in Washington, lay helpless all winter, and was finally ordered to Europe by my physician.[37]

other key activists, including Julia Ward Howe, author of the "Battle Hymn of the Republic," Lucy Stone, an opponent of slavery who shocked people of the day by using her maiden name instead of her husband's name, and Frances Willard, an early leader of the movement to prevent the abuse of drugs and alcohol. Barton, however, did not hate or scold men. As her biographer Ishbel Ross says, "Clara had worked too long and too closely with men under stress to feel that they were her natural enemies."[35]

5 The International Red Cross Seeks Barton's Help

In early 1869, suffering from sore throats, earaches, coughing, and rheumatism, Barton felt much older than her forty-seven years. When she received doctor's orders to go to Europe to regain her health, she knew she was financially able to fulfill his prescription. She had always jotted down her expenditures, to the last cent. She owned land in Iowa, and railroad investments were yielding dividends. She had become an independent woman with property, one who could afford to travel to Europe to recuperate.

She also had a friend abroad. Jules Golay, the Swiss volunteer who had helped her in Annapolis, had returned to Switzerland. She sent him $420 in gold to buy her ticket to Europe, guessing nothing of what her contact with his family would mean for her future. Then, accompanied by her sister Sally, Clara embarked on a summer sightseeing trip through Scotland. Sally returned home after touring Scotland, but Clara went on to Switzerland to see Jules and his parents, Isaac and Eliza Golay.

A delegation of Swiss gentlemen came to the Golay home in October 1869, with the special purpose of meeting Barton. The Golays had told them how the American woman had served in battle.

The delegates included Dr. Louis Appia, Henry Dunant, and other members of the International Committee for the Relief of the Wounded in War. They wanted to ask the visitor a question: "Why had the United States declined to sign the Treaty of Geneva providing for the relief of sick and wounded soldiers?" Although at the time Barton could only answer that she had never heard of the Treaty of Geneva, the question was to occupy her intensely between the years of 1876 and 1882.

Respecting the Sick and Wounded

While in Switzerland, Barton learned that at the same time she was on the battlefront in Virginia, people across the Atlantic Ocean in Europe had been reading *Souvenir of Solferina,* a book by Dunant that told how sick, wounded soldiers in the Franco-Sardinian War had been left without care. Dunant showed her a copy of the book, which he had written to tell of his volunteer nursing after a battle fought in Solferina, Italy, on June 24, 1859. The book had caused so much concern about neglect of the soldiers that it was translated and printed in several European languages. In Geneva, Switzerland, a committee had formed to support Dunant's proposal that belligerent nations begin to respect the sick and wounded. Dunant argued that soldiers who had put their lives on the line should not have to endure the additional suffering caused by the capture of their medical supplies. He thought that military ambulances should be immune from attack.

On February 9, 1863, Appia had taken Dunant's appeal before a summit meeting of the Congress of Berlin, where authorities from several European nations had gathered to discuss a recent treaty. A year later, sixteen nations, including Great Britain, France, Prussia, Spain, Austria, and Italy, sent delegates to an international conference at Geneva to study Dunant's proposal. Nations that signed the treaty Dunant proposed would allow volunteers to remove the wounded from combat zones without firing on them or taking them as prisoners. That is, they would treat sick and wounded soldiers of warring armies as neutrals.

Twelve of these sixteen nations gave their delegates power to sign the treaty, the first in a series of agreements now referred to as the Geneva Conventions. Their signatures authorized the formation of the International Association of the Red Cross, which would organize the needed relief. Although the United States had sent representatives to the convention, they had no authority to sign the treaty.

A Burning Question

Barton was deeply impressed that twelve nations had signed an international treaty because of the efforts of a few individuals. The more she heard about the Treaty of Geneva, the more she puzzled over why the United States had not agreed to its terms. She could only promise to look into the matter when she had become strong enough to return to her country.

The fulfillment of this promise was to be postponed, however—first for reasons of health. In Geneva the cold, windy winter worsened Barton's cough. In the spring, she left for the Mediterranean island of Corsica, but there too she failed to achieve either comfort or happiness. Her rooms were unheated and infested with fleas. Smoking chimneys inflamed her eyes and kept her from reading. She was too ill to think about the burning question of how to get the United States to sign the Treaty of Geneva.

Some change for the better came after she moved to a different hotel and was introduced to influential people in Corsica.

The signing of the Treaty of Geneva. One of the proposals under the treaty allowed volunteers to remove sick and wounded men from the battlefield without themselves being shot and killed.

Viewing there the birthplace and battle trophies of Napoléon I, Barton was carried back to her childhood memories of her soldier father and her Civil War service. From Corsica she went to Bern, Switzerland, for the steam baths. After that she made several trips to Geneva to learn about the Red Cross.

Barton Is Involved in the Red Cross Movement

In Bern Barton visited Red Cross storehouses full of bandages, food, and clothing. Volunteer workers were organized and ready, for in the spring of 1870 there were rumblings of war all over Europe. Here she saw clearly what careful preparedness might mean for the relief of wounded soldiers.

The grand duchess Louise, daughter of King Wilhelm of Prussia, was not content to let Barton rest. She sent for her on July 4, 1870, to come to Baden and learn how the Red Cross worked.

A group of Red Cross officials added their plea on July 10, saying that Barton's war experience would be useful to them. They would not let her say no, nor would they listen to her protests of poor health.

Though her doctors would surely have predicted that the decision would be fatal, Barton decided that to go would do her good. She was excited to think that she could both bring help to the soldiers and gain firsthand information she could use later for introducing the Red Cross into America. She was in Bern when the news came that Napoléon III had declared war on King Wilhelm on July 19, 1870. From then until the end of the Franco-Prussian

Napoléon III (pictured) declared war on King Wilhelm to start the Franco-Prussian War on July 19, 1870. During this time, Barton remained in Switzerland to gain firsthand knowledge of the International Red Cross.

War, on January 28, 1871, Barton observed the Red Cross in action.

Going to the Front with the Red Cross

Barton joined a French volunteer, Antoinette Margot, and her group. They left on August 8, 1870, carrying supplies to the war front along the Rhine River. In a later presentation on her work in France, Barton said:

As I journeyed on and saw the work of these Red Cross societies in the field, accomplishing in four months under their systematic organization what we failed to accomplish in four years without it—no mistakes, no needless suf-

Health Concerns

Biographer Ishbel Ross analyzes how Barton's health always seemed to be related to the intensity of the needs she perceived about her. Her eating habits seemed to have little to do with the requirements of her body.

"She dined largely on crackers and apples, which she usually carried with her on her journeys in brown-paper bags. Her fare was always frugal and austere. She avoided meat at different times in her life and periodically, if not consistently, was a vegetarian. After the Civil War her gastric [stomach] troubles drove her from one experiment to another.

She consulted many doctors, both men and women, in the course of her life but had periods when she avoided them altogether and threw out all her remedies. She got her best results from physiotherapy and the self-application of mental control."

Barton joined volunteer Antoinette Margot's (pictured) Red Cross group to carry supplies to the wounded along the Rhine River.

fering, no starving, no lack of care, no waste, no confusion, but order, plenty, cleanliness and comfort wherever that little flag made its way—a whole continent marshaled under the banner of the Red Cross. As I saw all this, and joined and worked in it, you will not wonder that I said to myself "if I live to return to my country I will try to make my people understand the Red Cross and that treaty."[38]

Barton's observations detailed the important concept of preparing for war in times of peace. The International Red Cross, already in operation for half a dozen years, had a large, well-stocked storehouse in Basel, Switzerland. There Barton saw a larger supply than she

had ever seen at any one time in readiness for the field at our own Sanitary Commission rooms in Washington, even in the fourth year of the war; and

Red Cross nurses aid the wounded during the Franco-Prussian War. The International Red Cross was an organized and prestigious organization while Barton observed it. Because supplies and training were obtained during peacetime, the organization was well prepared when called upon in times of crisis.

the trains were loaded with boxes and barrels pouring in from every city, town and hamlet in Switzerland, even from Austria and Northern Italy, and the trained, educated nurses stood awaiting their appointments, each with this badge upon the arm or breast, and every box, package or barrel with a broad bright scarlet cross, which rendered it . . . safe.[39]

In Basel she learned the organization of the storerooms and how they were filled, how the volunteers disbursed goods and arranged to travel to the lines of battle.

As Barton entered the war zone, she saw the Red Cross flag respected as a sign of neutrality. The volunteer group stopped in Paris, but Barton forged ahead to Strasbourg, where the French were under siege, and on toward Baden to meet Duchess Louise. She was taken prisoner at the border, but once she arrived, the duchess protected her. She served the wounded while the Prussian armies bombarded the besieged cities.

Work in Strasbourg

When Strasbourg surrendered on September 28, 1870, Barton entered with the German army and walked through the destroyed streets. In the short time since her first visit to the besieged city, immense devastation had swept over it. There were twenty thousand homeless—women and children who had lost fathers, sons, and husbands, many of them maimed, starving, and scarcely clothed.

The Red Cross relief efforts began immediately with well-organized breadlines. But, observing the despair of the defeated French, Barton soon developed a plan to help them regain their self-respect. She purchased bolts of cloth and found a place to set up a few cutting tables. Within a week 250 women were sheltered under an overhanging rock making patterns and cutting out clothing, which could be sewed at home and then sold for a small amount. Thus, people were clothed and could earn the means to feed their families at the same time. Later a building was adapted to contain the project. The grand duchess sent cloth, and her niece, Anna Zimmerman, joined Antoinette Margot in supervising the work.

In late December, after starting similar operations in other cities, Barton returned to Strasbourg for a month. One of a number of gratifying events was a surprise Christmas party, where the grateful people of the city brought her a huge

The Prussians bombard the French at Strasbourg (left). After the French defeat, Barton organized employment for French women with the help of Anna Zimmerman (above), the niece of the grand duchess.

Christmas tree covered with candles and fruit. Otto von Bismarck, the German nobleman with authority over the city, told her that he was pleased with her work and her ideas. The grand duchess Louise presented her and Anna Zimmerman each a Red Cross pin. And she had a visit from her friend Dorence Atwater, with whom she had worked on the Andersonville lists.

Relief Work in France

Soon after Strasbourg fell, Paris went under siege. When the French capital surrendered, on January 28, 1871, Atwater left for Paris. Barton followed with food and forty thousand garments made by the women of Strasbourg. She walked into the

Miss Barton Encourages a Seamstress

One of the women who sewed for the Strasbourg factory made uneven stitches and crooked hems yet wished to be paid the full amount. Barton's tact and gentleness show in this exchange, as recounted by Antoinette Margot in Daughter of Destiny *by Blanche Colton Williams.*

"[Miss Barton] took the two skirts, and examined the first in deep silence, her face showing not the smallest change of expression. . . . The woman seemed anxious and troubled, and she too was silent.

Every stitch of the first skirt was passed in review; she laid it down gently and took up the second skirt. When there remained only three or four inches of the large hem to complete the minute examination, she stopped. The woman started a little, and so did I, in apprehension. But Miss Barton's face looked pleased and encouraging; between her two thumbs she was holding carefully a very small bit of the hem, about a quarter of an inch long. 'What can it be?' thought I. At last Miss Barton spoke; 'Look, Madam, at these three stitches; how regular they are, how perfectly you have made them. Are you not glad of that little bit? I must say I could not make them prettier; they are very, very good. Are they not, Miss Margot?' she asked, turning toward me at her side. 'Yes, these three stitches are very good,' said I. . . .

'I see, Madam,' Miss Barton told the woman, 'you can sew very well, and I should not be surprised if next week your work were among the best we receive. It would certainly be today if it were all like these three stitches. I am full of hope for you, Madam.'"

city, for all the horses had been eaten for food, and told the mayor the Red Cross had arrived. All the relief work in Paris was done through the Red Cross, much of it under the direction of Barton. She and Mary Hinternach, a friend from Strasbourg, served the poor for six weeks from a small home. Barton did as much as she could but felt discouraged because the needs were so great. She noted particularly the needs of women, who often pulled loads that had been assigned to horses before the war. In summarizing the Red Cross work, Epler writes:

> History has recorded the sufferings, the horrors of misery, that accompanied and followed that siege, but history can never relate what wretchedness was averted, what multitudes of lives were saved by the friends and effort of the relief societies. What the State of France must have been without the merciful help of the Red Cross, imagination does not picture.[40]

One of Barton's major problems was to find ways to distribute supplies and money sent by Americans. Since the United States had not signed the Treaty of Geneva, there was no official channel for this relief and no one authorized to receive it. Before she left Paris she wrote out accounts for all she had distributed. She made a separate, extra report to tell the New York French Relief Committee how she had used the money the group had sent, all the while reflecting that if the United States had signed the Treaty of Geneva the relief would have been much more effective.

While Barton was helping with the relief effort, she felt stronger than she had for some years. She took time to write to

her family. She made it a point to see Americans who were in France. She spent five days with the Margot family. Here she sewed for herself and dressed up, after so many weeks of plainness. She was delighted when her friend Henry Wilson spent a day with her.

In the last two months of 1871, accompanied by Anna and Antoinette, Barton brought Red Cross food and clothing to the towns of northern France. Germany and France signed a peace agreement at Versailles, but the German army of occupation remained until 1873, when France, already impoverished by the war, had completed payments of its war reparations in the amount of two billion francs.

Recuperation

At the end of 1872 Barton returned to Strasbourg to rest and recuperate. Here she found that the families of her helpers Anna Zimmerman and Antoinette Margot objected to their extended participation in the relief effort. The visit turned into a time of illness. At fifty-one, Barton suffered from blindness, coughs, and weakness so severe she could hardly walk. To avoid pressuring the young women to accompany her, she returned to Paris. After she joined an American, Joseph E. Holmes, and his family, she revived enough to go sightseeing in Italy.

Returning at the end of May to Paris and London, Barton met with an American judge and his wife, Joseph and Abby Sheldon, who begged her to return to Washington with them. But she stayed on in England, seemingly determined to complete her doctor's three-years-in-

The Articles of the Treaty of Geneva

The Nine Articles of the Conference of 1863, which culminated in the signing of the Treaty of Geneva, lay the foundation for a system of relief societies for all the countries that joined in the agreement. Barton's summary of seven of the articles are included in Epler's Life of Clara Barton.

"The first naturally provides for the security of the hospitals in which the wounded might happen to be collected, that they shall be held neutral, and be respected by belligerents and that the sick or wounded remain in them.

Articles 2 and 3 provide for the neutrality and safety of all persons employed in the care of the wounded in hospitals, surgeons, chaplains, nurses, attendants, even after the enemy has gained the ground; but when no longer required for the wounded, they shall be promptly conducted under escort to the outposts of the enemy to rejoin the corps to which they belong, thus [preventing] all opportunity to roam free and make observations under cover of neutrality.

Article 4 settles the terms on which the material of hospitals, field and general, shall be regarded, that field hospitals shall not be subject to capture.

Article 5, with the view of quieting the fears of the inhabitants in the vicinity of a battle, who often flee in terror, as well as to secure their assistance, and the comfort of their homes for the care of the wounded, offers military protection and certain exemptions to all who shall entertain and care for the wounded in their houses.

Article 6 binds the parties contracting the Treaty not only to give the requisite care and treatment to all sick and wounded who fall into their hands, but that their misfortunes shall not be aggravated by the prospect of banishment or imprisonment. They shall not be retained as prisoners of war, but if circumstances admit, may be given up immediately after the action to be cared for by their own army, or if retained until recovered and found disabled for service, they shall be safely returned to their own country and friends, and that all convoys of sick and wounded shall be protected by absolute neutrality. . . .

Article 7 provides for hospital and convoys—an arm badge for persons. The design proposed was a red cross upon a white ground."

Europe prescription. Her London stay turned to misery with the coming of autumn and its cold days and damp rooms, but she seemed helpless to take the necessary steps to get well or go home. A brief interlude with the grand duchess in Baden cheered her, as did her thoughts of Henry Wilson, who had become the running mate of Ulysses S. Grant and was elected vice president of the United States for Grant's second term in 1872.

Finally, accompanied by the Sheldons, Barton embarked from Liverpool for New York toward the end of September 1873. On the way, she pondered her new vision of international cooperation and humanitarian treatment of prisoners, the sick, and the wounded. She wondered whether her country had room for her and her conviction that all nations needed to work together.

She arrived in the United States in October and was visiting her family in Oxford when her sister Sally died in Annapolis. Declining health plagued Barton from her sister's death in 1873 until after the death of Henry Wilson on November 22, 1875. Shortly thereafter, she entered the spa at Dansville, in western New York. In the sanatorium there, she began a daily healing routine of hot baths. It was at Dansville, in 1876, that she met a professor of chemistry in one of the city's schools, who was to become her most important staff member and colleague. Julian B. Hubbell had been fourteen years old when the Civil War started and had read in the newspapers of Clara Barton's courage in caring for soldiers on the battlefield. When he learned that she was living in Dansville, he came to see her.

At first Hubbell was shocked to see Barton on a sickbed, a woman in her mid-fifties, with graying hair. But her sense of humor drew him back to visit her often and to ask if he could help her in any way. It happened that she was giving a talk and needed a large wall map. He brought that and assisted at the lecture. Soon he was hearing about the Treaty of Geneva. Again he asked what he could do. This time, remembering that she would need a doctor on her staff, she told him, "Get a degree in medicine."[41] Hubbell immediately enrolled in the School of Medicine at Ann Arbor, Michigan.

After meeting Hubbell, Barton began to believe she could give serious attention to the question posed by the representatives of the International Committee for the Relief of the Wounded in War. In May she wrote to Louis Appia of her renewed energy. By July 4, 1876, she felt she was well enough to plan her move to Washington.

6 Barton Brings the Red Cross to the United States

Having begun her crusade for the Treaty of Geneva, Barton kept firmly to her course. Her strategy comprised two necessary preliminaries. She needed to communicate to the American people, and to their representatives in the Department of State and the War Department, the nature of the Red Cross movement, and then to establish a staff and organization that would be prepared to carry out its mission once the treaty was signed.

In the late 1870s Barton estimated that not one in five hundred Americans had any idea of the Red Cross. Yet she was certain that when they understood it, they would want to share its humanitarian work. In the government, very few knew anything about the treaty the United States had rejected in 1864. One who did know, Henry Bellows, had given up trying to convince the United States to sign.

As head of the War Department's Sanitary Commission during the Civil War, Bellows had sent a representative to the convention in Geneva. But the secretary of state, William Seward, had deemed the treaty impossible to sign while the country was divided in a civil war. Moreover, the Monroe Doctrine, which idealized noninterference and isolation, was the accepted guide in foreign affairs. Bellows could say nothing to sway the president and the sec-

retary of state from their conviction that the Monroe Doctrine's ban on "entangling alliances" applied to the Treaty of Geneva. Bellows believed that the situation was closed.

Clara Barton in the mid-1860s, around the time that she worked to bring about an American Red Cross.

The Patience of Miss Barton

Barton postponed her campaign to create the American Red Cross when she saw that the policies of Lincoln and Grant's Secretary of State William Seward were still championed by his son Frederick, who served with his father in 1864 and 1868 and again under President Hayes. Barton's account of this time appears in the biography by Percy H. Epler.

"I . . . saw how the fate of The Red Cross depended not alone on the Department but on *one man* [Frederick Seward] who was Assistant Secretary of State in 1864 and in 1868 when the Treaty had on two occasions been presented to our Government. It was a settled thing. There was nothing to hope from that [Hayes's] Administration. It would be decided because it had been decided. If I pressed it to a decision [there would be] a third refusal. I waited. My next thought was to refer it to Congress. That would be irregular and discourteous to the administration. I did not like to take it; still I attempted it, but could not get it considered as it found neither political patronage nor votes.

The next year I returned to Washington to try Congress again. I published a little pamphlet of two leaves addressed to the members and Senators to be laid upon their desks in the hope they would take the trouble to read so little as that. My strength failed before I could get the bills presented, and I went home again. There then remained but a portion of the administration and I determined to outlive it, hoping another would be more responsible. Meanwhile I wrote, talked and did whatever I could to spread the idea among the people."

Barton Presents the Red Cross to the U.S. Government

Unlike Bellows, Barton knew the Red Cross by firsthand experience. She felt hopeful that if she told how the Red Cross relieved needless suffering, she could succeed where Bellows's ten years of trying had failed.

Barton moved back to Washington, D.C., in October 1877. Once there, she published and distributed a four-page pamphlet, *What the Red Cross Is*, to provide basic information to the public. She also composed a plan for establishing a fully authorized relief organization. She argued:

Although we in the United States may fondly hope to be seldom visited by the calamities of war, yet the misfortunes of other nations with which we are on terms of amity [friendship] appeal to our sympathies; our southern coasts are periodically visited by the scourge of yellow fever; the valleys of the Mississippi are subject to destructive inundations [floods]; the plains of the West are devastated by insects and drought, and our cities and country are swept by consuming fires. In all such cases, to gather and dispense the profuse liberality [generosity] of our people, without waste of time or material, requires the wisdom that comes of experience and permanent organization.[42]

For three months she went around to department heads in the government to explain how the Red Cross worked. She left her pamphlet and a copy of the Geneva resolutions in the offices. She was sure that word of her work would reach the ears of President Rutherford B. Hayes.

Working the Social Angle

To further her cause Barton did what was necessary to get her name before the public. She had her portrait painted by society artist Mrs. Cornelia Adele Strong Fassett, and it was favorably judged in an art exhibition before being hung in the home of the consul general, John Hitz. When Mrs. Hitz held a reception for the unveiling in her home on New Year's Day 1878, Barton was present, wearing the same green velvet dress she had worn for the portrait sitting. As a result of this exposure, John D. Defrees, the head of the Government Printing Office, arranged an interview with President Hayes.

Barton's Promise Fulfilled

In 1882 Clara wrote to Gustave Moynier, president of the International Red Cross, to introduce to him some of her supporters. The letter appears in Epler's The Story of Clara Barton.

"All this [the signing of the Treaty of Geneva by the United States] had been accomplished, by the kindly help of a few personal friends, tireless and unremitting, and while the news of the accession of the Government of the United States to the treaty of Geneva, lit bonfires, that night (for I cabled at their request) in the streets of Switzerland, France, Germany, and Spain, a little four line paragraph in the Congressional doings of the day in the 'Evening Star,' Washington, alone announced to the people of America that an International Treaty had been added to their rolls. No formal distinction had been bestowed, no one honored, no one politically advanced, no money of the Government expended and like other things of like nature, it was left in obscurity to make its own way and live its own hard life."

On January 3 Barton met briefly with the president. She gave him an official letter of delegation from Gustave Moynier, the current president of the International Committee, repeating the invitation for the United States to sign the Treaty of Geneva. Hayes read the letter in her presence and said he would refer it to the secretary of state for decision.

After four days, with no word from the president, Barton dropped off her thank-you note, written January 4. The first stage of her work seemed to have achieved success, but she knew it would take great diplomacy and much care to reverse the previous decisions not to sign.

Unsuccessful Lobbying

Barton continued to write letters and speak with various officeholders. However, she knew that President Hayes had pledged to serve only one term and realized that the election of a new president might afford her a better chance of success. So Barton took a much-needed break.

A new president, James A. Garfield, was elected in 1880. Three days after Garfield's inauguration, Barton resumed her campaign by correspondence. Her letters now were written under the following letterhead: Red Cross, Office of Clara Barton, American Representative. Barton wrote to army generals asking for endorsements for her plan, including such well-known figures from the Civil War as Grant, Butler, P. C. Sheridan, A. E. Burnside, and W. S. Hancock. She also wrote to Elihu B. Washburne, the U.S. ambassador to France, whom she had met in Paris, asking him to use his influence with Presi-

President James A. Garfield showed interest in Barton's Red Cross idea and arranged to have her meet the secretary of state to further her plan.

dent Garfield to recommend the Treaty of Geneva. With the letters she sent copies of the letter to President Hayes and of the Articles of Confederation of the treaty. This treaty, she explained, would put the United States on a par with the other nations of the world, twenty-five in all, that had already signed it.

Within three weeks Barton caught the interest of President Garfield and was granted a long interview with the new secretary of state, James G. Blaine, who was so sympathetic to her cause that she felt she had accomplished her mission. After studying the Red Cross articles, however, Blaine concluded that the president alone could

The home of the first chapter of the American Red Cross in Dansville, New York.

not commit the country to the agreement because it was in the form of a treaty, and according to the U.S. Constitution, treaties must be approved by two-thirds of the Senate. Obtaining Senate approval would take time, but Barton was convinced that starting a Red Cross organization was important to the national character and prestige. Her determination did not waver.

The First Red Cross Organization in the United States

As soon as President Garfield showed initial interest, Secretary Blaine and Omar D. Conger, a Michigan judge, drafted a resolution to present to the Senate. This resolution, submitted on May 19, 1881, authorized the signing of the international treaty. Although the Senate had not yet voted, it seemed certain that the first session of the 47th Congress would grant a Red Cross charter. Barton sent out formal invitations for the purpose of organizing a central National Society of the Red Cross of Geneva. This group met on May 21, elected officers, and adopted a constitution that embodied the goals of the international organization.

In response to a joyful letter from Barton, Gustave Moynier wrote to Secretary of State Blaine thanking him for his willingness to consider the 1877 request that the United States become a signatory of the Treaty of Geneva. Moynier mentioned, as well, that four countries of the Western Hemisphere, Chile, Argentina, Bolivia, and Peru, had recently signed. All seemed well.

Treaty debate was put on hold once more, however, on July 1, 1881. President Garfield was shot in a railroad station by Charles J. Guiteau, a disappointed office seeker. The president lived on for just over two months, but died on September 19. As the nation waited to see whether the president would live, Barton continued to push her cause. She wrote articles and engaged a printer to make six thousand copies of one of her speeches, which she mailed around the country.

To honor Barton and the seventeenth anniversary of the Treaty of Geneva, the first local branch of the Red Cross was founded in Dansville during this interim. All the aims and objectives of the Red Cross were included in its charter, and dues were set at twenty-five cents a year, as reported in the Dansville *Advertiser* on August 25, 1881.

At the end of August a simple argument Barton had used in her pamphlet *What The Red Cross Is* became a prophecy. She had observed that war was not the only calamity that caused human suffering, noting that hardly a year goes by without floods, earthquakes, and the like. The hot, dry summer of 1881 had increased the fire hazard. In Michigan there were terrible losses from forest fires, raging out of control. A Michigan Relief Committee had been organized, but help from outside the state was needed.

Barton wrote to Julian Hubbell, still in medical school in Ann Arbor, asking him to go and assess the needs at the scene of the disaster. In Dansville she asked the new Red Cross organization to donate funds and clothing. Box after box of clothing was shipped to the Michigan Relief Committee.

Barton continued writing, producing a hundred-page book called *The Red Cross of the Geneva Convention*, a copy of which reached the New York *Sun*. The newspaper ran a prepublication review recommending the book and praising the author's preface, a letter entitled "To the People of the United States."

Success with the Secretary of State

In October 1881 Barton returned to Washington. She wrote Secretary Blaine that she had bought a hundred copies of *The Red Cross of the Geneva Convention* to circulate as soon as it came off the press. She also told him that two other Red Cross chapters had been formed, in Syracuse and Rochester, New York.

This aggressive publicity, and the honors Barton had received from other nations for her work with the Red Cross, encouraged Blaine to support the cause. The Gold Cross of Remembrance had been awarded in Alsace-Lorraine in 1871. Germany had bestowed the Iron Cross of Merit, and the grand duchess of Baden herself had placed around her friend's neck the Red Cross of Geneva in 1873.

On December 10, 1881, Blaine wrote to the new president, Chester A. Arthur, that he considered it advisable to adhere to this "international compact at once so humane in character and so universal in application."[43]

The Treaty Is Signed

The process of approval began when President Arthur sent the report of the secretary of state to the Senate Committee on Foreign Relations. Three thousand copies of the report were printed for publicity.

Before the 1881 Christmas holiday, the new secretary of state, Frederick T. Frelinghuysen, paid Barton the compliment of letting her hold, for a few moments, the official parchment copy of the treaty before it was signed by the president. But Barton had weeks of worry before the unanimous approval of the treaty by the Senate Foreign Relations Committee in February, its passage by the full Senate, and the actual signing on March 16, 1882.

Barton cabled the news to the International Committee in Switzerland, and they lit bonfires in the street in celebration. There were no celebrations in Washing-

---

Appeal to the American People

As soon as the treaty was signed, the Red Cross could name the U.S. government as party to its relief efforts. The first national appeal made by the American Association of the Red Cross, which appears in Daughter of Destiny, *was short and to the point.*

"The President having signed the Treaty of the Geneva Conference, and the Senate having, on the 16th instant, ratified the President's action, the American Association of the Red Cross, organized under provisions of said treaty, purposes [intends] to send its agents at once among the sufferers by the recent floods, with a view to the ameliorating [improving] of their condition so far as can be done by human aid and the means at hand will permit.

Contributions are urgently solicited. Remittances in money may be made to Hon. Charles J. Folger, Secretary of the Treasury, chairman of the board of trustees, or to his associates, Hon. Robert T. Lincoln, Sec'y of War, and Hon. George B. Loring, Commissioner of Agriculture. Contributions of wearing apparel, bedding, and provisions should be addressed to "The Red Cross Agent," at Memphis, Tenn., Vicksburg, Miss., and Helena, Ark.

Clara Barton,   Mrs. Omar D. Conger,
J. C. Bancroft Davis,   A. S. Solomons,
Frederick Douglass,   Mrs. S. A. Martha Canfield,
Alex. V. P. Garnett,   R. D. Mussey,
     Committee
Washington, D.C., March 23, 1882."

President Chester A. Arthur was instrumental in getting the United States to sign the Treaty of Geneva.

ton, D.C., however; no honors or publicity for the organization's American sponsor. The long wait and worry had left Barton depressed and wondering what she would do next. She called a meeting for the third week of March, to reorganize the national Red Cross according to its official congressional charter. She felt sure that her work had been done and prepared to resign.

First Work of the American Red Cross

Meantime, the season of Mississippi River floods had brought calls for help. Days after the meeting, by March 23, 1882, Barton changed her mind about resigning. The American Association of the Red Cross made its first national appeal for the relief of flood disaster with Barton's name heading the signatures of the relief committee.

7 Relief in Times of Disaster

The American Red Cross was established at a most opportune time. "The decades following the Civil War were rife with catastrophe," writes John S. Blay.[44] Barton had argued the need for a peacetime relief organization with news of floods and fires, drought and famine, tornadoes and hurricanes fresh in her mind. Such disasters continued for the next twenty years and occupied the American Red Cross with hundreds of opportunities for service.

The Michigan forest fires of 1881 were followed by the Mississippi and Ohio Rivers floods of 1882. Barton and the directors of local Red Cross chapters pooled their expertise to develop policies for the new organization. They decided never to ask for contributions but rather to stand ready to receive relief; not to pay officers a salary; to keep a stated sum on hand to make immediate service possible; to distribute immediately whatever was sent; and to account for the money and other donations as soon as relief had been finished.

Borrowed for the Prison System

With new policies in place, Barton settled into her task of supervision in the Washington office of the American Red Cross. At age sixty-two she was confident that her field-workers, headed by Hubbell, were serving the wounded and needy on the front lines as she had done in her Civil War days.

Red Cross volunteers aid victims of floods in Mississippi in 1882.

So when former Union general B. F. Butler, now governor of Massachusetts, begged her to interrupt her work at Red Cross headquarters in May 1883 and fill the position of superintendent of the Massachusetts Women's State Prison at Sherborn, she agreed to do it. Upon accepting the job, however, Barton found that she was also the secretary and the treasurer, and that her salary was half what the man who had preceded her as superintendent had received.

Barton undertook her work without complaint. Under her guidance the prison's supply rooms and dining halls were organized and cleaned. Barton downplayed punishment and, instead, encouraged good behavior, careful work habits, and personal responsibility. She was as successful and well liked among the inmates as she had been among her students. Nevertheless she resigned when Governor Butler left office, before she had completed a year in the position.

More Midwest Flooding

Barton returned to Washington from Sherborn, accompanied by Hubbell. Later, in *A Story of the Red Cross*, she wrote:

> Before we had even time to unpack our trunks, the news of the fearful rise of the Ohio River, of 1884, began to shock the country with its loss of life and property.

> I had never been present at a disaster in civil life. . . . But if by virtue of my office as president I was liable to be called every year to preside over and provide for them, it was essential that I

learn my duties experimentally. I accordingly joined Dr. Hubbell, who had been appointed general field agent, and proceeded to Pittsburgh, the headwaters of the rise.

> Telegraphing from there to our agents of the Associated Press, we proceeded to Cincinnati, to find the city afloat.[45]

A tornado that destroyed land routes followed, and then freezing weather. Barton chartered a riverboat, the *John S. Throop*, complete with crew and captain. The boat zigzagged down the river, leaving coal, food, and warm clothes with clergymen or other recognized leaders. The five-day trip to the flooded area near Cairo, Illinois, on the narrow tongue of land between the Mississippi River and the mouth of the Ohio River, was followed by a three-week return to the northern supply point, Evansville, Indiana, leaving grateful people all the way.

Preparations for relief down the Mississippi River centered in St. Louis, with the *Mattie-Bell* carrying workers and material for rebuilding homes and restarting the farms. Henry Sibley, a seed distributor, rushed $10,000 worth of seed to the Red Cross in Memphis so that farmers could replant.

Barton traveled up the Ohio River one time more aboard the *John S. Throop*. The work of helping stranded victims she described later in *A Story of the Red Cross*:

> Picture, if possible, this scene. A strange ship with a strange flag steaming up the river. It halts, turns from its course, and draws up to the nearest landing. Some persons disembark and speak a few minutes with the family. Then, a half dozen strong mechanics

Red Cross members, including Barton, sailed down a badly flooding Mississippi River in relief ships, including the Mattie- Bell *(second from right), to give aid to stranded victims of the flood.*

man a small boat laden with all material for constructing a one-room house —floor, roof, doors, windows. The boat returns for furniture. Within three hours the strange ship sails away, leaving a bewildered family in a new and clean house with bed, bedding, clothing, table, chairs, dishes, candles, a little cooking-stove with a blazing fire, all the common quota of cooking utensils, and meat, meal, and groceries; a plow, rake, axe, hoe, shovel, spade, hammer, and nails.[46]

In the four months of Mississippi and Ohio flood relief, cash donations had exceeded cost by a little over $1,000. This allowed Barton to send $800 to the New Orleans chapter for tornado relief in Louisiana and Alabama.

Clara was sixty-three years old on Christmas Day 1884. Looking back twenty years later, she noted she had "run all manner of risks and dangers, but had lost no life nor property, sunk no boat, and only that I was by this time too weak to walk without help—all were well."[47]

Delegate to Geneva

September 17, 1884, was the opening day of the Fourth International Conference of the Red Cross, the first to which the United States, as a signatory to the treaty, sent delegates. Secretary of State Frelinghuysen asked Barton to head the first official U.S. delegation to the conference, held in

Cincinnati and the Flood of 1884

In A Story of the Red Cross, *Barton reported on conditions in Cincinnati after the flood that gave her one of her first experiences in domestic relief operations.*

"[The] inhabitants were being fed from boats through the second-story windows. These conditions were telegraphed. Supplies commenced to flow in, not only from our own societies but from the people of the country. Warehouses were filled, in spite of all we dispensed—but there were four hundred miles of this distress—even to Cairo [Illinois], where the Ohio, sometimes thirty miles in width, discharged its swollen waters into the Mississippi.

Recognizing this condition lower down the river as the greater need, we transferred our supplies and distribution to Evansville, Indiana. Scarcely had we reached there when a cyclone struck the river below, and traveling up its entire length, leveled every standing object upon its banks, swept the houses along like cockle-shells, uprooted the greatest trees and whirled them down its mighty current—catching here and there its human victims, or leaving them with life only, houseless, homeless, wringing their hands on a frozen, fireless shore—with every coal-pit filled with water, and death from freezing more imminent than from hunger.

There were four hundred miles more of this, and no way of reaching them by land. With all our tons of clothing, these people and their homeless little children were freezing. There was but one way—the Government boats had come with rations of food—we too must take to the water."

Red Cross volunteers float down the streets in Cincinnati in boats during the flood of 1884.

Geneva. The Senate appropriated funds for her and two others: A. S. Solomon, vice president of the American Red Cross, and Judge Joseph Sheldon, who had been her friend since 1870.

Barton followed her report to the conference with a request "that under the Red Cross Constitution of the United States its national organization should be permitted to act in the capacity of Red Cross relief agents, treating a national disaster like a field of battle."[48] Not only was her request granted, but provisions for rendering aid in disasters other than war were placed in the international treaty. This addition came to be known as the American Amendment, and after its ratification it was included in the charters of several other countries.

A Standing Fund

As Barton now saw the Red Cross role in relief work, the organization would have experienced help, essential supplies, and authority to inform the public of the seriousness of each disaster that required its assistance. Red Cross workers would direct the distribution of all relief sent and stay at the disaster site as long as needed.

But there remained a flaw in the organization's structure. The Red Cross, Barton realized, could not guarantee prompt and complete assistance without a standing fund. For example, $80,000 worth of relief was distributed in the Michigan forest fire disaster. But for this immense effort to begin, Red Cross members had to put up their own money until donated money and supplies began coming in from the American public. Even a later

gift of $3,000 from Barton to the Red Cross did not go far as the organization's standing fund.

Three Major Disasters

Three major disasters during the years 1886 to 1889 proved conclusively to Barton that to be able to offer aid immediately, before donations could arrive, the Red Cross needed a substantial standing fund. The organization helped with relief operations amounting to $100,000 in 1885–1886, alleviating hunger in Texas after three years of drought. Similar conditions in Russia brought about a famine there, and U.S. donors sent generous contributions in 1891. In New Hampshire, as Barton reports it, the Mount Vernon tornado

> cut a broad swath through the eastern half of the town, destroying everything in its path, tearing down brick houses, uprooting trees, and picking up small wooden houses and carrying them along as if they were made of cardboard. . . . In a very few minutes after the storm had passed, the sun shone out brightly, but on what a scene! The air was filled with cries of anguish coming from the maimed sufferers crushed under the ruins, and with the wailings for the dead and missing.[49]

After two weeks of Red Cross relief, people took up their lives again.

A yellow fever epidemic in Florida in the summer and autumn of 1888 helped the Red Cross to refine its techniques for dealing with a "plague" situation. Without understanding that mosquitoes carried the disease, nurses who had become im-

Members of the Red Cross arrive at the scene of the Johnstown Flood to help its victims. Listed as the worst disaster of the nineteenth century, the flood tested the mettle of the still-new organization.

mune through previous infection were eager to help. They had learned how to keep people from dying of yellow fever. The Red Cross hired these nurses because their skill discouraged people from fleeing a yellow fever town and spreading infection to other places.

Red Cross disaster techniques were tested after May 31, 1889, the day of the Johnstown Flood, listed as the worst U.S. disaster of the nineteenth century. Johnstown, Pennsylvania, is located at the junction of the Little Conemaugh River and Stone Creek; in 1889 its population of thirty thousand lived below a seventy-foot dam. The lake behind the dam covered many acres. The worst-case scenario came to pass when heavy rains fell all over west-

ern Pennsylvania and the dam, which was known to be unsafe, broke, releasing a fifty-foot wall of water to tear through the city.

The next day, June 1, 1889, Red Cross relief was on site. Barton's twenty-page history of the Red Cross in Johnstown does not tell of the numberless memorials to her efforts, but it does suggest the magnitude of the disaster:

> For five weary months it was our portion to live amid these scenes of destruction, desolation, poverty, want and woe; sometimes in tents, sometimes without; in rain and mud, and a lack of the commonest comforts, until we could build houses to shelter ourselves and those around us. Without a

Two photos dramatize the effects the Johnstown Flood had on the city. At left is a picture of Main Street following the flood. The picture at right shows a tree that was driven through the upper story of a building by the force of the floodwaters.

safe, and with a dry goods box for a desk, we conducted financial affairs in money and material to the extent of nearly half a million dollars.

I shall never lose the memory of my first walk on the day of our arrival—the wading in mud, the climbing over broken engines, cars, heaps of iron rollers, broken timbers, wrecks of houses; bent railway tracks tangled with piles of iron wire; among bands of workmen, squads of military, and getting around the bodies of dead animals, and often people being borne away—the smouldering fires and drizzling rain . . . to announce that the Red Cross had arrived.[50]

As Barton often said, the Red Cross was people responding to people's needs. Its role was to ensure fair and selfless administration of the generous donations of money and goods that poured in to a disaster area. At the close of 1889, $3,000, the amount Barton had deposited in the Red Cross account, had been replaced and was once again available. Operating honestly and efficiently, with almost no funds of its own, the Red Cross could deliver thousands of dollars worth of aid.

Hurricane in South Carolina

The last great civil relief work in which Clara Barton participated before the end of the century took her back to the scene of Civil War suffering at the time of the siege of Charleston, South Carolina. A hurricane and tidal wave devastated the Sea Islands at the mouth of Charleston Bay in August 1893. Barton said she would

leave the descriptions of this fearful catastrophe . . . to the reports of those who saw, shared its dangers and lived within its tide of death. They will tell how from 3,000 to 5,000 human beings . . . went down in a night; how in the blackness of despair they clung to the swaying tree tops till the roots gave way, and together they were covered in the sands or washed out to the reckless billows of the great mad ocean that had sent for them; of the want, woe and nothingness that the ensuing days revealed when the winds were hushed, the waters stilled and the frightened survivors begun to look for the lost home and the loved ones, and hunger presaged the gaunt figure of famine that silently drew near and stared them in the face. How with all the vegetable growth destroyed, all animals, even to fowl, swept away, all fresh

The Work of Relief in South Carolina

The March 1894 issue of Scribner's Magazine *included Joel Chandler Harris's report about the hurricanes that battered the Sea Islands, whose population consisted largely of former slaves. Harris's article told how the marshes could be penetrated only by boats. Loss of the boats delayed Barton's relief work.*

"Miss Barton had some experience with . . . this region in the first months after the war, and therefore had nothing to learn or to unlearn. . . . Her name was known to the older ones, and one old negro woman—Aunt Jane—who had cooked for her 'when freedom come 'bout,' came thirty miles to see her.

But with all its experience, with all its energy and discipline, the Red Cross Society was compelled to move slowly. . . . It could not give boats to its messengers nor wings to its messages. All that it could do was to launch some of the boats that had been blown ashore, and hire others that had been rescued. Presently, too, the negroes began to recover some of their own boats that had been lodged in the marshes, and then the work of organizing relief committees on the islands began. It was slow and tedious. The delay was almost disheartening. Malarial fever was playing havoc with the destitute—not killing them outright, but so weakening them as to cause death from the lack of nourishing food or from exposure; for hundreds were living in the bushes, practically without shelter, and hundreds were without clothes."

water turned to salt,—not even a sweet well remaining—not one little house in five hundred left upright, if left at all; the victims with the clothing torn and washed off them, till they were more nearly naked than clothed.[51]

Barton brought makeshift Red Cross headquarters to Beaufort, on the South Carolina mainland, on September 5, 1893. She chartered a warehouse and set up her office. From this office she began to meet the needs of which a Beaufort resident, Adm. Lester Anthony Beardslee, wrote:

> There are 30,000 American citizens who must be almost entirely supported by charity until they get a spring crop in April or May. Unless they are furnished with food they will starve, without bedding they will die from exposure; without medicines, of fever. Everything not perishable is needed, especially money to buy lumber, nails, bricks and hardware to rebuild houses, cast-off and warm clothing, cooking utensils, pans, pots, spoons, etc.[52]

Barton's report in *The Red Cross: A History of This Remarkable Movement in the Interest of Humanity* tells how many houses the Red Cross built on each island in Charleston Bay and how much flooded land was drained by ditches or flood walls. Red Cross workers established communications through intricate channels of marshland. They taught people to build little fences around their gardens to protect them from the pigs, to cut and plant potatoes, and to use seeds they had not seen before—lettuce, carrots.

Clothing was needed for men, women, and children. But what was sent, Barton said, was "very largely . . . for women and children."[53] In addition, much of the donated clothing was useless until it had been "mended, strengthened and put into proper condition."[54] Barton established sewing circles so the women could repair and remake the clothing.

Barton left Charleston and her work on the Sea Islands July 24, 1894. The gratitude of the people for the restoration of shelter and cultivation were symbolized to Barton by the gift of one of the Sea Island villages, recalled in *A Story of the Red Cross:*

> Their thanks they had emphasized and proved by the heavy basket that Jackson, their representative, had carefully brought all the forty miles. It contained seventy-one fresh eggs—the gift of seventy-one families—being a contribution of one egg from each family, from the day or two previous to his leaving.[55]

8 American Red Cross, International Emissary

The decade from 1891 to 1901 expanded Barton's understanding of international relief operations. It was one thing, she found, to send help to Russia after crop failures in 1889–1890. It was a quite different matter to give relief to a country enmeshed in civil war. The Red Cross easily obtained free transportation for cargo that supported seven hundred thousand starving Russians for a month in 1891. But many delicate negotiations were necessary before the Red Cross could even enter Turkey and Cuba, whose citizens were fighting each other inside their respective countries.

Moreover, in her middle seventies, Barton was beginning to hear objections to her leadership style. Some of her younger staff members thought her administration of the Red Cross too autocratic and individualistic. Their feelings were expressed publicly in the March 1895 issue of the *Review of Reviews*. The author, freelance writer Sophia Wells Royce Williams, said that something so important as the Red Cross needed

a national organization, a national board, and reports which would stand as model and guide for all relief work, the country over. . . . [Instead] . . . [t]he country has Miss Clara Barton, industrious, indefatigable [tireless],

persistent and enthusiastic. . . . For thirteen years since the United States signed the Geneva Convention the National Red Cross Association in this country has been Miss Clara Barton and Miss Clara Barton has been the National Red Cross Society.[56]

That summer, perhaps by way of response, Barton tried to draw at least one millionaire corporate leader, George M. Pullman, of the Pullman Palace Car Com-

An elderly Barton faced criticism of her leadership of the Red Cross. Many felt it was time for Barton to retire and allow a national board to fill her place.

pany, into her circle of leaders. He declined, but his nephew, George H. Pullman, offered his personal assistance.

Red Cross Relief in Turkey

Barton decided to accept the younger Pullman's offer when the American Board of Foreign Missions, in September 1895, asked Barton to take relief to Armenians in Turkey, south and east of the Black Sea. Missionaries had reported massacre and destruction in that mountainous region.

Although Turkey had signed the international Treaty of Geneva in 1865, Turkish officials thirty years later hesitated to recognize Red Cross neutrality. The Ottoman rulers in Turkey, who considered themselves to be putting down an uprising, opposed American aid. The Turkish political situation was made more difficult by religious conflict between the largely Christian Armenians and the Turks, who followed Islamic law.

In America, writes Epler, "It was conclusively seen that the International Red Cross alone could reach a zone so jealous of interference of other nations. Non-political,

Charity as a Business Transaction

After the Armenian relief effort Barton was asked whether the Red Cross was "embarrassed" by the lack of funds collected. In Clara Barton: A History *Barton recounts her answer.*

"We were never embarrassed in our operations by lack of funds, holding, as I always have, that charitable relief in order to be safe and efficient, should be conducted on the same reasonable basis as business, and that a good businessman, unless by accident on the part of other persons, or of circumstances, will never find himself embarrassed, as he will never undertake more than he has the means to successfully accomplish. We were never embarrassed in our operations by lack of funds, and our committees will testify that no intimation of that kind ever came to them from us. . . . But if asked if we had enough for the needs of the people, enough to relieve the distress through desolated Asia Minor, enough to make those people comfortable again, then a very tender chord has been touched. No hearts in America are more sore than ours; its richest mine might drain in that attempt. Our men in the interior have seen and lived among what others vainly strive to picture; they are men of work, not words, and under heaven have labored to do what they could with what they had."

non-sectarian, it could enter where no army could pass."[57] But even in America, which had almost no Muslim population, anti-Turkish sentiment blocked much of the fund-raising.

Barton was well aware that Red Cross immunity did not automatically extend to those who brought aid for victims of a revolution. Nevertheless, with Hubbell, Pullman, and a small staff, she sailed for Constantinople, determined to find a way to use Red Cross neutrality in the service of the Armenians. She later wrote in her report that

> only by abstaining from discordant opinions could we be in a position to perform our work. By the obligations of the Geneva Treaty, all national controversies, racial distinctions, and differences in creed must be [suspended] and only the needs of humanity considered. In this spirit alone can the Red Cross meet its obligations as the representative of the nations and governments of the world acting under it.[58]

All the way across the Atlantic, Barton wondered whether they would be allowed to land in Constantinople. While the ship docked briefly in England, Hubbell went ahead alone to arrange a meeting with the U.S. minister to Turkey, Alexander W. Terrell, representatives of the missionary board, and the Turkish minister of state, Tewfik Pasha.

At the meeting Terrell said that the American people wanted to relieve "the suffering condition of the people of the interior in consequence of the massacres."[59] Barton listed the relief supplies—farming tools, seed wheat, and harvesting implements—and insisted that the Red Cross

would not be spying or aiding insurgents. Furthermore, she stated, "Such as I give I shall expect to receive."[60] Barton's review of the meeting continues:

> Almost without a breath [Pasha] replied, "We honor your position and your wishes will be respected. Such aid and protection as we are able to, we shall render."
>
> I then asked if it were necessary for me to see other officials. "No," he replied, "I speak for my government"; and with cordial good wishes, our interview closed.
>
> I never spoke personally with this gentleman again; all further business being officially transacted through the officers of our Legation. Yet I can truly say . . . that here commenced an acquaintance which proved invaluable, and here were given pledges of mutual faith of which not a word was ever broken.[61]

During her six months in Constantinople, Barton directed four Red Cross relief expeditions into the Armenian territory that was under Turkish rule. Aid to two hundred villages slowed the spread of deadly diseases: typhoid, typhus, dysentery, and smallpox. Thousands of refugees resumed planting, rebuilt their homes, and made clothing. Scythes, sickles, and threshing machines were collected or improvised for the harvest. Cattle that had been driven away were rounded up or repurchased with $22,000 sent especially for this purpose. There were no riots or disturbances. Barton described an atmosphere of "friendship, comradeship, confidence, and love . . . among newly found friends."[62]

Red Cross workers use clubs to ward off those interfering with their efforts to evacuate Armenian war victims.

Misunderstanding and Opposition

The home headquarters, however, was trying to explain conflicting reports about the expeditions and to defend the Red Cross against criticism. One pro-Turkish newspaper article accused a pro-Armenian group of "working hand in glove with Miss Clara Barton and the Red Cross Society."[63] Pro-Armenian reports suggested that delayed delivery of relief supplies to Armenians and a change in the expedition route from the Black Sea to the Mediterranean were evidence of Red Cross bias in favor of the Turks.

Barton heard both sides in Constantinople—the needs of the people in Armenia, and the criticism from Turkish and Armenian supporters in the United States. In the center of controversy and conflict, she wrote:

> Here was a singular condition of affairs. A great international work of relief, every department of which was succeeding beyond all expectation, wherein no mistakes had been made,

letters of gratitude and blessing pouring in from every field of labor, finances carefully handled and no pressure for funds. On the other hand a whole nation in a panic, strong committees going to pieces, and brave faithful officers driven through pity to despair and contempt, and the cause about to be abandoned and given up to the lasting harm of all humanity.[64]

Realizing that her staff at headquarters could not stand up under the criticism, she canceled all Red Cross collection of relief in the United States.

Return Home and International Convention

When Barton left Constantinople the Turkish government conferred upon her for "humanitarian, scientific and other services of distinction" a rare and prestigious honor documented by a diploma written in Turkish, and much cherished by its recipient.[65] She arrived back in New York on September 12, 1896.

After a rest, Barton traveled to Vienna as the U.S. delegate to the Sixth International Conference of the Red Cross, in September 1897. Her report to the conference showed that U.S. chapters led all others in delivery of relief. Her leadership solidified the expansion of the Red Cross mission beyond war to natural disaster. This expansion of the Red Cross mission continues today.

On her return Barton settled in her office building at Glen Echo, Maryland, outside Washington. From here, she thought, she could direct the American Red Cross in peace and comfort.

Barton was not to enjoy her peaceful office setting for long. By the end of 1896 she could not ignore the news of suffering caused by Cuba's struggle for independence from Spain. Guerrilla warfare, which had been growing fiercer for over ten years, was threatening the Spanish government. The Spanish rulers detained women and children in concentrated areas, or camps, to keep them from helping Cuban revolutionaries. Since more and more people were either taking up arms or being detained, few farmers were left to raise crops, and the detainees, called *reconcentrados*, were starving. Calls for relief came from these Cuban victims of civil war.

As this "new murmur fast growing to clamor" came to Barton, she reviewed the politics of the United States in relation to its southern island neighbor.[66] The president of the International Red Cross, Gus-

---

Red Cross Headquarters

The Red Cross home office, where Barton hoped to work in peace after returning from Turkey, is described by biographer Ishbel Ross, as it looked in the 1950s.

"The house is a white clapboard building, with two steeple-roofed turrets, one of which had a vault built into it for the protection of Red Cross documents. The interior suggests a ship, with its long central hall, its paneled walls, railed balcony, and apartments opening off both floors. Three penthouse rooms are set in the lantern roof, and tinted light streams in through the colored glass of its Red Cross windows. The balcony railing was traditionally hung with Clara's international flags. Oriental rugs, silks, trophies of various kinds from different parts of the world showed up against the dark paneling. A gold settee from the Grand Duchess Louise and an onyx-topped gold-leaf table were among her treasures. Today Glen Echo still has the huge oak desk on which she wrote so many letters, made countless diary entries, and transacted much of her Red Cross business."

tave Moynier, cautioned her that international law still did not protect groups or individuals, even from neutral countries, if they entered colonies in rebellion. The United States was a neutral nation, but some American investors were deeply involved in Cuba's export of sugar, tobacco, and coffee. President William McKinley did not want to alienate them. Neither did he want to alienate Americans who favored Cuban freedom.

Spain could, of course, send its own Red Cross, but this did not happen. And, to make matters worse, some prominent American Red Cross chapter members were not waiting for diplomatic agreements. Not only were they organizing relief shipments in the name of the Red Cross; they were accusing Clara Barton and the American Red Cross of withholding help. By sending relief without clearance, they were violating the Red Cross charter and opening up the possibility that Red Cross helpers would be fired upon. The relief supplies of these maverick groups were being confiscated, just as they would have been in Turkey if Barton had neglected to make the proper arrangements.

By July 12, 1897, Barton had heard enough about how she was obstructing Red Cross relief to Cuba. In this international crisis she decided to utilize for the first time the full official Board of Consultation provided by the 1881 congressional charter. This board included the U.S. president and the department heads of the army and navy. At Barton's request, President McKinley convened a meeting, after which the president and secretary of state, with Spanish approval, authorized relief for the *reconcentrados* and made the Red Cross its official distributor.

On February 6, 1898, Barton sailed to Havana with three hundred tons of supplies: quinine (for the treatment of malaria), rice, cornmeal and potatoes, canned meat and bacon, fruit, and malted milk. Her diary of her first week in Havana, February 9–15, 1898, contains this description of her visit to a *reconcentrado* camp:

> [O]ver four hundred women and children in the most pitiable condition possible for human beings to be in, and live, and they did not live, for the death record counted them out a dozen or more every twenty-four hours, and the grim, terrible pile of rude black coffins that confronted one at the very doorway, told to each famishing applicant on her entrance what her existence was likely to be.[67]

Barton with physicians and nurses in front of the clinic at Havana. Determined to clear her reputation, Barton made every effort to aid the victims in the war between Cuban nationals and Spain.

Barton organized her stores immediately and worked in the central warehouse. Since many people could not obtain fuel, bakers were hired to make bread from the flour. The people were given tickets, which they presented for bread and food.

The *Maine*

While in Cuba, Barton had lunch with Capt. Charles D. Sigsbee aboard the U.S. Navy battleship *Maine*. The *Maine* had arrived in Havana harbor in January 1898 for military exercises and to remind Spain of U.S. interests in Cuba. Joined by William Willard Howard, a New York newspaper reporter, Barton met several of the two hundred sixty sailors aboard. For the next two days Howard and Barton recorded donations in the makeshift Red Cross office on shore. In her history of the Red Cross, Barton recalls that they were at work late the night of February 15, 1898, when

> suddenly the table shook from under our hands, the great glass door opening onto the veranda, facing the sea, flew open; everything in the room was in motion or out of place—the deafening roar of such a burst of thunder as perhaps one never heard before, and off to the right, out over the bay; the air was filled with a blaze of light, and this in turn filled with black specks like huge spectres [ghosts] flying in all directions. Then it faded away. The bells rang; the whistles blew, and voices in the street were heard for a moment; then all was quiet again. I supposed it to be the bursting of some

Charles D. Sigsbee was captain of the Maine *when it was sunk on February 15, 1898. The sinking started the Spanish-American War.*

mammoth mortar, or explosion of some magazine. A few hours later came the terrible news of the *Maine*.[68]

The mysterious explosion that destroyed the *Maine* and killed most of its crew surprised everyone. Investigations by both Spain and the United States failed to disclose the person or persons responsible.

After the destruction of the *Maine*, Spanish authorities cooperated with Barton until her withdrawal from the island following the U.S. announcement of a naval blockade of Havana. The blockade went into effect on April 9, and all U.S. citizens were ordered to leave the country.

Even with the blockade in force, President McKinley gave Barton authority to charter a ship, the *State of Texas*, to take new collections of relief to the *reconcentrados*. By the time the United States had declared war on Spain, on April 29, the *State*

MAINE EXPLOSION CAUSED BY BOMB OR TORPEDO?

Capt. Sigsbee and Consul-General Lee Are in Doubt---The World Has Sent a Special Tug, With Submarine Divers, to Havana to Find Out---Lee Asks for an Immediate Court of Inquiry---260 Men Dead.

IN A SUPPRESSED DESPATCH TO THE STATE DEPARTMENT, THE CAPTAIN SAYS THE ACCIDENT WAS MADE POSSIBLE BY AN ENEMY.

Dr. E. C. Pendleton, Just Arrived from Havana, Says He Overheard Talk There of a Plot to Blow Up the Ship--- Zalinski, the Dynamite Expert, and Other Experts Report to The World that the Wreck Was Not Accidental---Washington Officials Ready for Vigorous Action if Spanish Responsibility Can Be Shown---Divers to Be Sent Down to Make Careful Examinations.

A headline proclaims the destruction of the Maine. *Although it has never been determined who destroyed the* Maine, *the United States declared war on Spain as a direct result of the explosion.*

of Texas was loaded at Key West, Florida, with fourteen hundred tons of food and other supplies. But even the president's authorization would not convince the captain of the battleship *New York* to let Barton proceed against the U.S. blockade, which had been ordered to keep all shipments of food out of Havana.

In *A Story of the Red Cross,* Barton recalls the scene during her seven weeks' wait in Key West: "[T]he fleets of war, and the [navy's] stately glistening white ships of relief that dotted the sea . . . and among them one inconspicuous, black-hulled sea-going craft, laden with food for the still famishing *reconcentrados,* when they could be reached."[69]

The *State of Texas* was allowed to sail for the Caribbean on June 20, but not the hundred miles to Havana where the *reconcentrados* awaited Barton's help. Rather, the vessel was directed around the island to Cuba's far southeastern coast "where the marines had made a landing and were camped on the shore."[70]

Upon arriving in the waters off Siboney, near the southern port of Santiago de Cuba, the Red Cross workers waited at anchor for another week. When the *State of Texas* was finally given clearance to dock at Siboney, the arrival was bittersweet, for the *reconcentrados* remained four hundred miles away.

Meanwhile the armies of the United States and Cuba were trying to capture Santiago by taking the hills behind it since the city's supply of fresh water originated in the hills. On June 27, 1898, news reached the Red Cross ship that Theodore Roosevelt's elite unit, the Rough Riders, had taken the first strategic spot, Kettle Hill. From the deck of the ship Barton watched soldiers setting out on the jungle march of eight or nine miles toward the next objective, San Juan Hill.

State of Texas, *the relief ship of the American Red Cross that attempted to cross the naval blockade to bring supplies of food and medicine to the* reconcentrados.

Teddy Roosevelt's Rough Riders ride to victory during the Spanish-American War. (Below) Barton and her nurses aid the wounded in Cuba. During the battle of San Juan Hill, Barton's nurses were kept busy attending physicians in the operating room of a small hospital.

That night she and three Red Cross women went ashore in a small boat. At the army camp they found the hospitals under the control of Gen. Calixto García of the Cuban forces. García was eager for Red Cross help, but American officers said that the soldiers' hospital was no place for women. Even García said the Red Cross workers should wait until the hospital was in better order. Nevertheless, Barton writes in *A Story of the Red Cross,*

> [the women] at once went to work, thoroughly cleaned the little three-room building—García's abandoned headquarters, to be used as a hospital—and when the day closed the transformation showed clean rooms, clean cots, and the grateful occupants wondering whether heaven itself could be more comfortable, or anything more desirable than the palatable [tasty] food prepared for them.[71]

Another Red Cross hospital was established and "scores of soldiers who had been lying on the filthy floors of an adja-

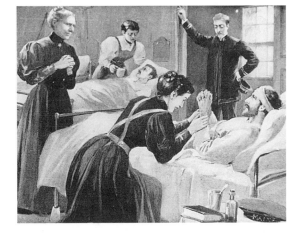

cent building, with no food but army rations, were carried over, placed in clean cots, and given proper food."[72]

By Friday, July 1, the little hospital was filled to overflowing from the ongoing battle of San Juan Hill, and all too soon there was too much work for the women to do. They worked in the operating tent for thirty hours without a pause. "We heard no more," Barton said, "about a woman nurse being out of place in a soldiers' hospital."[73]

U.S. general William Shafter (below) ordered Barton and her nurses (left) to deliver supplies meant for the reconcentrados to U.S. soldiers who were out of food and medicine.

By the second night of the battle for San Juan Hill, the army ran out of food and medicine. Taking advantage of wartime privileges, Gen. William Shafter ordered Barton to deliver to his men the Cuban Relief Committee supplies intended for the *reconcentrados*. Barton, in her concern for the American soldiers, cooperated with Shafter. She and her crew worked all night loading and unloading, ship to boat to wagon, paying Cubans who helped them with food, and then catching a ride with a farmer for the four-hour trip to the army camp. She brought two other loads of food to the front.

The eight hundred men at the field hospital grounds were cold, naked, and hungry, lying in mud and campfire smoke. Barton writes:

> The land was perfectly level: no drainage whatever; covered with long, tangled grass; skirted by trees, brush and shrubbery; a few little dog tents not much larger than could have been made of an ordinary table-cloth thrown over a short rail, and under these lay huddled together the men fresh from the field or from the operating-tables, with no covering over them . . . and in the majority of cases no blanket under them.[74]

President McKinley Commends the Red Cross and Barton

In his message to Congress on December 6, 1898, President William McKinley reviewed the Spanish-American War and his country's victory, which deprived Spain of her last three colonies, the Philippine Islands, Cuba, and Puerto Rico, transferring them to the protection of the United States. Barton quotes McKinley in A Story of the Red Cross.

"It is a pleasure for me to mention in terms of cordial appreciation, the timely and useful work of the American Red Cross, both in relief measures preparatory to the campaigns, in sanitary assistance at several of the camps of assemblage, and, later, under the able and experienced leadership of the president of the society, Miss Clara Barton, on the fields of battle and in the hospitals at the front in Cuba. Working in conjunction with the governmental authorities and under their sanction and approval, and with the enthusiastic cooperation of many patriotic women and societies in the various States, the Red Cross has fully maintained its already high reputation for intense earnestness and ability to exercise the able purposes of its international organization, thus justifying the confidence and support which it has received at the hands of the American people. To the members and officers and all who aided them in their philanthropic work, the sincere and lasting gratitude of the soldier and the public is due and freely accorded."

President William McKinley had nothing but praise for Barton and her nurses during the Spanish-American War.

Just as in Civil War days, Barton built a better fireplace, found kettles and a tarpaulin to protect the food, and cooked bucket after bucket of thin cereal out of flour, salt, condensed milk, and cornmeal. Hearing stories in the drizzling rain of soldiers who had gone into battle hungry, Barton "felt that it was again the same old story and wondered what gain there had been in the last thirty years."[75]

Relief Work Continues

After another day at camp the Red Cross joined Cuban and U.S. Army surgeons and nurses in the hospital. Because the soldiers had stormed a hill, facing fire from above, there were many head wounds to care for. The *State of Texas* went after a load of ice. Every fast-melting chip helped save some soldier's eyesight or kept him from fever.

Soon after the Spanish surrendered San Juan Hill, General Shafter entered into truce negotiations. *A Story of the Red Cross* tells about Shafter's treatment of prisoners:

The Spanish soldiers had been led by their officers to believe that every man who surrendered—and the [civilians] as well—would be butchered whenever the city should fall and the American troops should come in. But when General Shafter commenced to send back convoys of captured Spanish officers, their wounds dressed, and carefully placed on stretchers, borne under flags of truce to the Spanish lines at Santiago, and set down at the feet of General Toral, . . . a lesson was learned that went far toward the surrender of that city.[76]

Shafter thus became one of the first to practice the humanitarian principles of the International Red Cross treaty by exchanging prisoners rather than keeping them as hostages.

As soon as the Spanish flag was lowered, July 17, 1898, Barton entered Santiago harbor with the twelve hundred tons of food still on her ship. Relief efforts in Santiago continued through August 13, when peace was confirmed, and for several days afterwards. A second Red Cross ship, the *Clinton*, was chartered. It arrived in Havana, but Barton did not unload it because no government was in place. Instead, over several months, she visited various villages and islands of Cuba, delivering what relief she could and refusing to succumb to either age or weariness.

From a later perspective Barton recalled:

Cuba was . . . full of heart-breaking memories. It gave the first opportunity to test the cooperation between the government and its supplemental handmaiden, the Red Cross. That these relations might not have been clearly understood at this initial date may well be appreciated, but that time and experience will remedy this may be confidently hoped.[77]

9 When Letting Go Means Letting Grow

On her return to Red Cross headquarters Barton was forced to confront changes taking place within the organization that she had founded. Red Cross officers and board members had gradually come to view the organization, its volunteer staff, and funding in ways Barton found difficult to accept. Barton did not agree with many of the changes being sought, so for her the years 1900 to 1904 were filled with turmoil.

During her later years, Barton was constantly bombarded by calls for change from members of the American Red Cross who wanted younger leadership.

At first the internal conflict seemed to center around Barton's decision in 1898 to give American soldiers donated goods intended for needy Cubans. Several of Barton's board members thought she had too easily complied with the general's order. They worried about possible damage to Americans' trust in the ability of the Red Cross to get donations to the people for whom they are intended. They felt her action signaled that at age seventy-nine she might be too old to direct an organization that could command such large sums of money and supplies.

Barton's age was not the only issue for her younger coworkers. Some of them believed that the Red Cross needed new leadership—preferably young, influential corporate executives. They also felt that the organization needed to broaden its leadership base so that it did not have to rely on the ideas and energy of one person. One board member, Mabel T. Boardman, felt the organization would receive greater respect and be better served by having a man at the top.

Other concerns also surfaced. Some Red Cross board members argued that the only way to attract top leadership was to offer high salaries. Office staff also began to insist on being paid for their work. Up until this point, most Red Cross workers, including Barton, had volunteered their time, and Barton had always viewed the Red Cross as an all-volunteer agency. These and other demands and suggestions marked a change in philosophy for the organization.

Barton knew that her time as head of the American Red Cross was limited, but she was torn between wanting to resign and feeling that the organization was not yet ready to go on without her guidance and know-how. Financing continued to be a major concern for Barton. She had been arguing for decades that it was impossible to gather enough money and support for international wartime operations from volunteer sources alone. To be most effective, Barton announced, the Red Cross would need a standing account of at least one million dollars. This money would allow the Red Cross to maintain constant preparedness for wartime and disaster relief. The money could be obtained through corporate grants and private donations or endowments. Agreeing at last to the changes sought by Barton, Congress passed a bill on June 6, 1900, allowing the Red Cross to establish an endowment fund. The bylaws were changed to include a new Board of Control to oversee financial outlays. With another successful effort behind her, Barton begged to resign. Her resignation was not accepted, but several positions on the new Board of Control were filled by people who opposed her ideas.

It took only a few weeks for Barton to see that after years of self-direction, it would go against her grain to ask the Board of Control about every expenditure. She took the first opportunity to return to the field and reassert her ideal of active, working leadership.

Respite in Fieldwork

Barton's last fieldwork followed a hurricane and tidal wave that struck Galveston, Texas, on September 8, 1900. She writes in *A Story of the Red Cross:*

> Here again, no description could adequately serve its purpose. The sea, with fury spent, had sullenly retired. The strongest buildings, half standing, roofless and tottering, told what once had been the make-up of a thriving city. But that cordon of wreckage skirting the shore for miles it seemed, often twenty feet in height, and against which the high tide still lapped and rolled! What did it tell? The tale is all too dreadful to recall—the funeral pyre of at least five thousand human

Red Cross headquarters in Galveston, Texas, in 1900. Barton's last fieldwork was performed in this city after a tidal wave and hurricane wreaked vast destruction.

beings. The uncoffined dead of the fifth part [20 percent] of a city lay there. The lifeless bodies festering in the glaring heat of a September sun told only too fatally what that meant to that portion of the city left alive. The streets were well-nigh impassable, the animals largely drowned, the working force of men diminished, dazed, and homeless. The men who had been the fathers of the city, its business and its wealth, looked on aghast at their overwhelmed possessions, ruined homes, and, worse than all, mourned their own dead.[78]

Relief Procedures

For three months Barton joined forces with the New Orleans Red Cross Society to meet the needs of Galveston, assisted by her nephew Stephen, of the Central Cuban Relief Committee, and Fred L. Ward, its secretary. Under their direction the Red Cross party implemented its well-learned procedures.

A Story of the Red Cross reports that the aid workers visited the entire area, noting what buildings were usable for storage of supplies, what transportation routes could be used when "broken houses, cars, wagons, church steeples, and grand pianos were liable to be encountered in the middle of the leading streets, themselves buried three feet in the coarse black sand."[79]

Assistants met the refugees, filled their immediate needs for food and suitable clothing, and kept records. After that, writes Barton, "Homes must be made, lumber obtained, and houses built."[80] Up to ten thousand were estimated dead, and

A photo reveals the incredible destruction in Galveston following a tidal wave and hurricane in 1900. Red Cross workers rebuilt homes, buried the dead, and gave food and supplies to the wounded and homeless.

burial was impossible. People living in tents had no employment. Families in suspense still hoped for their loved ones' return.

The Opposition Continues

Barton's return to Red Cross headquarters in December 1900 intensified the clash of opinions there. The office secretary insisted on a salary, while Barton had asked for and received nothing for her work in the field. The Board of Control requested a complete report on the Galveston relief, imposing an impossibly short deadline for its completion. Barton spent her eightieth year at the office, continually feeling at odds with the monetary policies of the Board of Control.

Political issues became even more difficult to resolve when President McKinley was shot on September 6, 1901, and died a

Devastation in Galveston

In A Story of the Red Cross, *Barton tells of the difficulties of transporting relief supplies to refugees of the Galveston hurricane.*

"Bridges had been swept away, and new sand-bars thrown up in the bay; floating roofs and timbers impeded navigation, and the only method of communication between the mainland and Galveston was one poor little ferry-boat, which had to feel her now dangerous way very cautiously, by daylight only. She had also to carry nearly a quarter of her capacity in soldiers to prevent her being swamped by wailing crowds of people, frantic to learn the fate of their friends on the island. Each trip to the mainland, the boat came filled with refugees from the city of doom—the sick, the maimed, the sorrowing—many with bodily injuries inflicted by the storm, and others with deeper wounds of grief—mothers whose babies had been torn from their arms, children whose parents were missing, fathers whose entire families were lost—a dazed and tearless throng, such as [the Italian poet] Dante might have met in his passage through Inferno. These were dumped by thousands on the sandy beach at Texas City, and then conveyed by rail to Houston, to be cared for by the good people of that city, who, notwithstanding their own grievous losses, were doing noble work for their stricken neighbors."

This schoolhouse was carried six hundred feet by floodwaters from the Galveston, Texas, tidal wave.

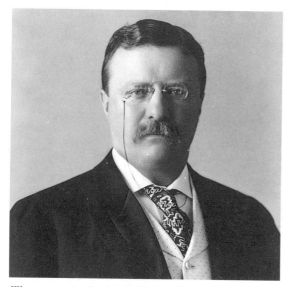

The aggressive foreign policies of President Theodore Roosevelt were at odds with the international goals set by the American Red Cross.

week later. The new president, Theodore Roosevelt, was committed to policies that made Red Cross neutrality and immunity difficult. The concept of manifest destiny, for example, entailed open maneuvers to obtain foreign military bases.

Despite the conflict within her organization, Barton remained a favorite at public functions. She did not expect official government recognition, but it meant a lot to her that she was enthusiastically cheered when she sat next to Roosevelt at a meeting of the Spanish[-American] War Veterans' Convention. She was the only woman seated at the president's table for a banquet, and she received more applause than the country's highest elected official.

At the Second Annual Meeting of the National Red Cross on December 10, 1901, Barton's supporters, with the help of her old friend Dorence Atwater, abolished the Board of Control. Again, at this meeting, she begged to be retired, but

since the meeting room was full of the personal supporters who had helped abolish the Board of Control, her resignation was rejected.

Seventh International Conference

Barton continued as the highest authority in the Red Cross. She was the official U.S. emissary to the Seventh International Conference in St. Petersburg, Russia, which discussed the naval treaties that would regulate hospital ships and prisoners taken in battles at sea. The Red Cross pamphlet *Clara Barton* credits her "personality and prestige" with influencing the conference proceedings, which were finally concluded five years later in 1907.[81]

After Barton's return from St. Petersburg, she took a few weeks to write and publish *The Story of My Childhood*. Then she braced herself for the next annual meeting. By December 9, 1902, she was torn between depression and feelings of fear for the organization.

The focus of the growing rift on the board of directors as summarized by one biographer, Williams, came to this:

> Briefly, the minority recognized a vast international system, of which America was but a member, a body in which no particular person—founder, organizer, or president—held peculiar rights. The majority recognized the same international system, with control vested primarily in Clara Barton, founder, organizer, President.[82]

The majority group was convinced that the Red Cross would survive without

Barton's personal leadership in the field. They wanted more people in the central administration and more separation between administrators and field staff. Barton's own long career reflected a mixing of the two. As always, she wanted the work of administration to be closely connected with fieldwork. For another biographer, Epler, the issues centered around leadership:

> The opposition was planning for the time when no such figure as Clara Barton in her vigor would exist.
>
> It was hard for her to understand this because the air was beclouded with personal charges on her own side and on the other which made her feel that it was necessary in defending herself to defend the old system of centralized authority and action in the President.
>
> Her modest and natural simplicity never let her once feel but what some new Clara Barton could arise to embody the spirit of the Red Cross and swing the country as she did. Those behind the new system knew this succession was impossible.[83]

At the 1902 board of directors meeting a roomful of supporters all prepared to cast proxy votes for other supporters. They passed a controversial amendment to the bylaws. The amendment increased the power of the president and centralized her authority. Then Barton was elected president for life.

Critics who had been members of the abolished Board of Control questioned Barton's ethics in the management of a piece of Red Cross property in Indiana. This land, which she had purchased for a dollar from Dr. Joseph Gardner and Enola Lee Gardner, was to have been the site of a new national headquarters building and Red Cross park. It had been placed in charge of a caretaker, John Morlan, who added his voice to the opposition with the complaint that he had not received the pay he had been promised. Once Morlan's complaint came to the front, the opposition centered their attention on Barton's handling of funds and records. They passed a motion to appoint an internal committee to investigate their charges.

After the 1902 meeting members of the board of directors, including Mabel T. Boardman, Sara Spencer, and J. Ellen Foster, sent a letter of protest to President Roosevelt. They claimed that Barton had misused her power as Red Cross president. Their letter stated that at the last meeting Barton had presented "an entirely new set of by-laws, repealing and superseding all other by-laws."[84] Because of

Mabel Boardman, a member of the board of directors of the American Red Cross, was one of those instrumental in forcing Clara Barton's resignation as president.

the changes, they said, President Roosevelt's integrity would be compromised if he served on the Board of Consultation. Later they also complained that Barton had mismanaged Red Cross funds. To emphasize their dissatisfaction with Barton's leadership, several members of the board of directors resigned.

A copy of the eight-page protest letter to Roosevelt was sent to Barton January 2, 1903, by George B. Cortelyou, the secretary to the president.

Barton answered the charges in a letter to President Roosevelt dated January 7, 1903. She pointed out that nothing had really changed since President Chester A. Arthur and the entire executive and legislative branch had fully endorsed the 1881 charter as handed to them in accord with the Treaty of Geneva. She noted that all the presidents since Arthur had served on the Board of Consultation. The Red Cross, after all, existed as a result of an international treaty and all was in order within the treaty's guidelines. She offered a public apology if she had erred. No further comment came from the White House.

Investigation

The investigaton committee that the organization had voted to set up called for reports on all handling of funds and properties, reports that had to be made at Red Cross expense and by Red Cross staff. Barton spent most of 1903 compiling these reports, calling it a "hard and terrible year."[85] The investigation concluded on May 3, 1904. The committee found that Morlan had written letters requesting a pension, which Barton had not granted. In light of the former caretaker's mismanagement of the property, these requests were now seen to amount to blackmail. A summary by the investigation committee listed "no charges of dishonesty or misappropriation of funds of any kind or character, the charges being limited to alleged want of a proper system of bookkeeping."[86] The committee was satisfied that Barton had kept as good financial records as were possible under circumstances of makeshift offices and dire human need.

Resignation

On May 12, 1904, a week after the committee issued its report, Clara Barton resigned her presidency. Her friend Mrs. John A. Logan, vice president, took over the chief administrative duties.

This was the setting in which Barton wrote A Story of the Red Cross, published in 1904, as a final letting go of her great work. Cleared of all charges, she admitted that her bookkeeping method may not have been "business-like . . . nor one to be approved by stated boards of directors nor squared by bank regulations. But the foes we had to meet were not thus regulated, and had to be met as they came."[87]

Following the December 1904 meeting, over which Mrs. Logan presided, Congress again asked for reincorporation and reorganization of the Red Cross, partly in response to new provisions in the most recent treaty protocols. The officially recognized volunteer relief society of the United States now had clearer lines of authority in government supervision; in addition, nonprofit status was assured for fund-raising purposes, and an officer of the War Department was assigned to audit the accounts. Thus the organization continued, much as Barton had mapped out the project in 1882. To the present, the Red Cross mission is defined by the federal government, but the organization receives no federal money.

Last Works

The year after her retirement from the Red Cross, Barton founded a new organization, the National First Aid Society. She directed local groups in the training of volunteers who gave safety instructions and taught fire departments and other civic groups how to bandage wounds, rescue drowning people, and stop bleeding.

Healthy and vigorous, Barton continued to be active through her eighty-ninth year. Still interested in Susan B. Anthony, she attended the suffragists' 1906 convention in Baltimore. Anthony, two years older than Barton, was ill and died a month later. In February 1908 Barton attended a memorial service for the naval men who had died on the *Maine*. She participated in a Memorial Day procession. She worked on a manuscript to follow the story of her childhood. A statement praising her work was published in 1910, following her attendance at a Masonic Hall reception June 17. Continuing her lifelong devotion to her relatives, she traveled to California to visit a cousin who was a clergyman, William E. Barton. This four-week visit, Williams says, "would have put to bed or buried a woman twenty years younger."[88]

Back at her house at Glen Echo, Maryland, she continued her independent ways, milking her cow, churning butter, cooking and cleaning, riding her horse Baba, read-

After her resignation, Barton spent quiet hours in her home in Glen Echo, Maryland, working the land and reading.

Recognized by Susan B. Anthony and the Suffragists

In Daughter of Destiny, *Blanche Colton Williams quotes a passage from Barton's diary. In it, Barton writes about her attendance at the Washington meeting of the suffragists on April 17, 1904.*

"I went to the platform amid cheers. Miss [Susan B.] Anthony had my place reserved beside her. Mrs. [Carrie] Catt presided. Anna Howard Shaw was the newly elected President.

Miss Anthony desired me to speak. I utterly declined. She then drew me beside her to the front of the stage and stood there with her arm about me while she told the audience that I was at the first suffrage meeting in Washington, in 1867, that later I sent out my call to the soldiers to stand by women as I had stood by them—that there were left now only us to stand together at this meeting tonight.

I said a few words and sat down. Miss Anthony spoke *one* minute and came back and we remained together till the close. We both realized that we should never stand together again before a Washington audience. . . . This was Providence's triumph for the night of 1867, which I so well remember."

Although Barton never actively pursued the equal rights of women, Susan B. Anthony (pictured) recognized Barton as an example of all that a woman could be.

ing about current events, grieving the death of friends younger than she. She cooperated with writers who wrote sketches of her life. She named as her authorized biographers two clergymen, her friend Percy H. Epler and her cousin William E. Barton. She proofread and corrected for Epler an article he had written about the men and women of Worcester County.

She was glad, at last, to take time to develop her spiritual life. She visited the founder of Christian Science, Mary Baker Eddy, and other spiritualists and mediums who practiced in Washington. Her interest in communication with the dead and life after death inspired long letters, including one to recommend a spiritualist to her friend the grand duchess.

As she began to prepare for her own death, Barton took the same orderly approach to that event as to any relief operation. Having caught cold in the early months of 1912, she became weaker and seemed to realize she would not recover her strength. She wrote her will, called Hubbell to be with her, and deeded her house to him. She wore her pins and decorations. Basically unafflicted by disease, clear in her mind, she resignedly gave up her activities. Hubbell stayed with her until she died, on April 12, 1912, three and a half months after her ninetieth birthday.

Hundreds came to the funeral in Oxford, Worcester County, Massachusetts. School children crowded the gallery of Memorial Hall, where the services were held. The grand duchess sent a wreath of green laurel. Epler led the funeral service. Soldiers stood at attention while the Grand Army of the Republic Auxiliary presented a silk flag. The procession, led by color bearers, bore Barton's body to the North Cemetery. The Rev. William E. Barton and seventeen other relatives were present for the graveside ceremony, all placing red roses on the grave.

After Barton's death the national press printed scores of comments on the simplicity of her character and her heroism on the battlefield. She received twenty-one honors and decorations, votes, thanks, and commendations. Later, in Meriden, Connecticut, on May 26, Dorence Atwater's son, Francis, gave the address at a final memorial. These ceremonies were published in a booklet that described Clara Barton as Founder of the American National Red Cross, President of the National First Aid Association of America, and President of the Alumnae Association of the Philadelphia School for Nurses. Hubbell wrote: "She will be in history the greatest of American women if not the greatest in the world."[89]

Beyond the Symbol to Ideal and Action

The importance of Clara Barton, as another century opens, reaches beyond the organization she founded. Her ideas and commitment live on in the 1.4 million volunteers who annually give of themselves when their neighbors near and far need help. Through their American Red Cross chapters they protect victimized persons, on land or sea, in wartime, and during national disasters. They promote humanitarian treatment of prisoners of war and civilians alike. And, like Barton, they minister to the most basic human needs—bandaging wounds, providing soup and bread, erecting tents, and building houses.

Preparedness

Barton firmly believed that there are no victors in war. But she also understood that war—at least for now—is a part of human existence and that the suffering caused by war is worse when preparations have not been made to see to the victims' many needs.

So, Barton argued, even when no danger of war exists, peacetime preparedness is the ideal. Those who volunteer readily and share generously when there are no hostilities may even open the way to

A young Barton wears a button with the symbol of the Red Cross, the American organization which she founded.

peacetime cooperation. The stocking of warehouses with food, the establishment and maintenance of emergency networks, the mustering of volunteers—these constitute the great work of peace that the Red Cross continues. Today, emergency networks, blood programs, organ donation, and AIDS education carry the Red Cross beyond the vision of the 1800s.

Community—the sense of caring, neighborly support—is formed by such preparedness. The memory of community sustains any, such as the soldier, who are away from home. The Red Cross worker brings as much community as is possible to the soldier on the front. To the victim of flood or earthquake or fire or other disaster, the Red Cross provision of temporary shelter, blankets, clothing, and hot meals speaks of the community that sent this aid. As Barton saw, resources such as food, medicine, and clothing are the deciding factor in the restoration of the victims' lives. Barton herself had few personal resources. Yet, by giving of herself, she supervised the use and expenditure of thousands of dollars and much-needed goods donated by caring individuals.

Barton as Personal Emissary

Through her many years of providing emergency and humanitarian aid, Barton developed strong views about how an or-

ganization could best serve those in need. Barton firmly believed that an officer in the Red Cross ought to have experience in the field. She believed, also, that Red Cross officers should not be paid. She believed that to be most effective, relief had to be immediate and spontaneous. Yet, as she worked with countless victims of disaster, she began to realize that the government must be involved.

The reorganization of the Red Cross after Barton's resignation produced more governmental structure and connections. As the organization grew, it became clear that fieldwork and office work had to be separated. Officials and staff needed salaries. Yet the appeal of the Red Cross remains a moral and personal one. The image of this intrepid woman nursing on the battlefield or visiting the offices of presidents and secretaries of state remains a symbol for the Red Cross worker today.

Barton always relied on logic and good sense in the achievement of her goals. She

---

A Woman of Many Talents

In her preface to Daughter of Destiny, *Blanche Colton Williams lists the many sides to Clara Barton's versatile personality and varied career.*

"Teacher, accountant, seamstress, laundress, cook, dairymaid; . . . Patent Office clerk, Civil War nurse, searcher for missing men after that war; . . . lecturer, originator of the plan at [Strasbourg] for rehabilitating . . . Franco-Prussian War sufferers; founder of the American Red Cross, founder of the First Aid Department of the American Red Cross; visitor, hostess, diarist, speaker, author of innumerable reports, author of *The Red Cross in Peace and War, A Story of the Red Cross* and *The Story of My Childhood* as well as many occasional verses. In short . . . a life of action . . . a life that stands of and by itself."

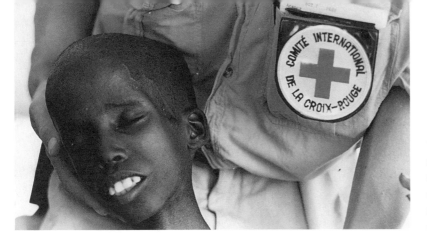

The Red Cross continues its relief efforts across international borders. It was instrumental in giving relief to recent famine victims in Somalia.

never left anything entirely up to people at the top. She succeeded because she met the policy makers eyeball to eyeball. She showed that one woman with neither money nor power can communicate her vision to the leaders of the world community.

Writing, speaking, campaigning, and lobbying in Washington, Barton went beyond direct service to analysis of patterns of action in the larger picture. She probed the causes of pain and injustice. Carrying in her heart the plight of men, women, and children, who had lost loved ones, home, clothing, sustenance, and life itself, she proposed solutions. She established a community of compassion in a world of violence and alienation.

What is apparent even today is that Barton's method still works, in small ways as well as large. What is required now, as then, are individuals willing to take responsibility, without counting the cost, for achieving the goals they set for themselves.

Barton as World Citizen

The Red Cross is committed to the ideal that each person who volunteers humanitarian relief promotes world understanding. Representing this ideal is Red Cross nurse Mary Taylor, who signed up for a field position in Somalia in 1993 with the Geneva-based International Committee of the Red Cross. Relief work bringing food to the famine-stricken people reduced the number of children dying per day from one hundred down to thirty. "I wouldn't be here if I thought it was hopeless," Taylor says.[90]

Kasandra Milne is another Red Cross volunteer. She leaves a supportive husband at home in Calgary while she distributes food aid in southern Sudan or Bosnia, countries torn by civil war.

Milne—and the other dozen Canadian Red Cross volunteers in the region—travels often in Bosnia's free-fire zones, but she is typically self-effacing about the danger she faces. "In most situations you are so busy reacting that by the time you have time to be afraid, it's history," she says.[91]

Clara Barton, through personal example, shows today's world citizen how to help. Basic needs such as food, shelter, and medical care remain unmet in many places, and war and political strife continue to ravage the populations of many nations. There is much to be done.

Notes

Chapter 1: A Precocious Child in an Ambitious, Close-Knit Family

1. Clara Barton, *The Story of My Childhood.* 1907. Reprinted, New York: Arno Press, 1980.
2. Clara Barton, *Story of My Childhood.*
3. Clara Barton, *Story of My Childhood.*
4. Clara Barton, *Story of My Childhood.*
5. Clara Barton, *Story of My Childhood.*
6. Clara Barton, *Story of My Childhood.*
7. Quoted in Clara Barton, *Story of My Childhood.*

Chapter 2: A Successful Teacher Moves on to Washington, D.C.

8. Quoted in William E. Barton, *The Life of Clara Barton*, 2 vols. Boston: Houghton Mifflin, 1922.
9. Quoted in William E. Barton, *Life of Clara Barton.*
10. Quoted in William E. Barton, *Life of Clara Barton.*
11. Blanche Colton Williams, *Clara Barton: Daughter of Destiny.* Philadelphia: Lippincott, 1941.
12. Williams, *Daughter of Destiny.*
13. Williams, *Daughter of Destiny.*
14. Williams, *Daughter of Destiny.*
15. Quoted in Williams, *Daughter of Destiny.*

Chapter 3: Behind the Lines in the American Civil War

16. Quoted in William E. Barton, *Life of Clara Barton.*
17. Ishbel Ross, *Angel of the Battlefield: The Life of Clara Barton.* New York: Harper & Brothers, 1956.
18. Quoted in William E. Barton, *Life of Clara Barton.*
19. Quoted in William E. Barton, *Life of Clara Barton.*
20. William E. Barton, *Life of Clara Barton.*
21. Percy H. Epler, *The Life of Clara Barton.* New York: Macmillan, 1917.
22. Quoted in Epler, *Life of Clara Barton.*
23. Quoted in Epler, *Life of Clara Barton.*
24. Quoted in Epler, *Life of Clara Barton.*
25. Quoted in Epler, *Life of Clara Barton.*
26. Quoted in Epler, *Life of Clara Barton.*
27. Quoted in Epler, *Life of Clara Barton.*
28. Quoted in Epler, *Life of Clara Barton.*

Chapter 4: Missing Soldiers and a National Memorial

29. Quoted in Charles Sumner Young, *Clara Barton: A Centenary Tribute.* Boston: Richard G. Badger/Gorham Press, 1922.
30. Quoted in Williams, *Daughter of Destiny* (from facsimile of original, Library of Congress).
31. Quoted in Ross, *Angel of the Battlefield.*
32. Quoted in Ross, *Angel of the Battlefield.*
33. Epler, *Life of Clara Barton.*
34. Quoted in Epler, *Life of Clara Barton.*
35. Ross, *Angel of the Battlefield.*
36. Ross, *Angel of the Battlefield.*
37. Quoted in Epler, *Life of Clara Barton.*

Chapter 5: The International Red Cross Seeks Barton's Help

38. Quoted in Epler, *Life of Clara Barton.*
39. Quoted in Epler, *Life of Clara Barton.*
40. Epler, *Life of Clara Barton.*
41. Quoted in Williams, *Daughter of Destiny.*

Chapter 6: Barton Brings the Red Cross to the United States

42. Quoted in Williams, *Daughter of Destiny.*
43. Quoted in Williams, *Daughter of Destiny.*

Chapter 7: The American Red Cross: People's Help for National Necessities

44. John S. Blay, *After the Civil War: A Pictorial Profile of America from 1865 to 1900.* New York: Bonanza Books, 1960.

45. Clara Barton, *A Story of the Red Cross: Glimpses of Field Work.* 1904. Reprinted, New York: Appleton, 1968.

46. Clara Barton, *Story of the Red Cross.*

47. Clara Barton, *Story of the Red Cross.*

48. Clara Barton, *The Red Cross: A History of This Remarkable International Movement in the Interest of Humanity.* New York: American National Red Cross, 1898.

49. Clara Barton, *The Red Cross: A History.*

50. Clara Barton, *The Red Cross: A History.*

51. Clara Barton, *The Red Cross: A History.*

52. Quoted in Clara Barton, *The Red Cross: A History.*

53. Clara Barton, *The Red Cross: A History.*

54. Clara Barton, *The Red Cross: A History.*

55. Clara Barton, *Story of the Red Cross.*

Chapter 8: American Red Cross, International Emissary

56. Quoted in Ross, *Angel of the Battlefield.*

57. Epler, *Life of Clara Barton.*

58. Clara Barton, *The Red Cross: A History.*

59. Quoted in Clara Barton, *This Remarkable Movement.*

60. Clara Barton, *The Red Cross: A History.*

61. Clara Barton, *The Red Cross: A History.*

62. Clara Barton, *The Red Cross: A History.*

63. Quoted in Clara Barton, *The Red Cross: A History.*

64. Clara Barton, *The Red Cross: A History.*

65. Quoted in Clara Barton, *The Red Cross: A History.*

66. Clara Barton, *Story of the Red Cross.*

67. Clara Barton, *The Red Cross: A History.*

68. Clara Barton, *The Red Cross: A History.*

69. Clara Barton, *Story of the Red Cross.*

70. Clara Barton, *Story of the Red Cross.*

71. Clara Barton, *Story of the Red Cross.*

72. Clara Barton, *Story of the Red Cross.*

73. Clara Barton, *Story of the Red Cross.*

74. Clara Barton, *Story of the Red Cross.*

75. Clara Barton, *Story of the Red Cross.*

76. Clara Barton, *Story of the Red Cross.*

77. Clara Barton, *Story of the Red Cross.*

Chapter 9: When Letting Go Means Letting Grow

78. Clara Barton, *Story of the Red Cross.*

79. Clara Barton, *Story of the Red Cross.*

80. Clara Barton, *Story of the Red Cross.*

81. American Red Cross, *Clara Barton: Heroic Woman.* American Red Cross pamphlet 570/322091. Washington, DC: ARC, 1982.

82. Williams, *Daughter of Destiny.*

83. Epler, *Life of Clara Barton.*

84. Mabel T. Boardman, *Under the Red Cross Flag at Home and Abroad.* Philadelphia: Lippincott, 1915.

85. Quoted in Williams, *Daughter of Destiny.*

86. L. A. Stebbins, "Sketch of the Investigation into the Affairs of the American National Red Cross," quoted in Williams, *Daughter of Destiny.*

87. Clara Barton, *Story of the Red Cross.*

88. Quoted in Williams, *Daughter of Destiny.*

89. Quoted in Williams, *Daughter of Destiny.*

Epilogue: Beyond the Symbol to Ideal and Action

90. "Samaritan in Somalia," *People Weekly,* December 28, 1993.

91. Vince Beiser, "Kasandra Milne: Compassion Under Fire," *Maclean's,* December 27, 1993.

For Further Reading

Clara Barton, *A Story of the Red Cross: Glimpses of Field Work.* 1904. Reprinted New York, Appleton, 1968. Readable and lively account of Red Cross activity from 1882 to 1904.

————, *The Story of My Childhood.* 1907. Reprinted New York: Arno Press, 1980. Barton's autobiography, written in response to the requests of many school children for information on her early life.

Mabel T. Boardman, *Under the Red Cross Flag at Home and Abroad.* Philadelphia: Lippincott, 1915. Continues story of the Red Cross from 1904 to 1915. Downplays Barton's role.

Robert Paul Jordan, *The Civil War.* Washington, DC: National Geographic Society, 1969. Many color pictures and much artwork with specific citations for each.

John McElroy, *This Was Andersonville.* Roy Meredith, ed. Illustrated by Arthur C. Butts IV. New York: Bonanza Books/ Crown Publishers, 1957. Modernized version of book first published in 1876, which was expanded from McElroy's newspaper accounts published in 1866.

Richard B. Morris and James Woodress, eds., *A House Divided: The Civil War, 1850–1865: Voices from America's Past.* St. Louis: Webster, 1961. Excerpts from writings of people living at the time.

Jeanette Covert Nolan, *The Story of Clara Barton of the Red Cross.* Illustrated by W. C. Nims. New York: Junior Literary Guild/Julian Messner, 1941. Fictionalized biography.

Fletcher Pratt, *The Civil War.* Illustrated by Lee J. Ames. Garden City, NY: Doubleday, 1955. Sixty-five-page young people's account of the war. Many comic book–type illustrations.

Additional Works Consulted

American Red Cross, *Clara Barton: Heroic Woman*. American Red Cross pamphlet 570/332091. Washington, DC: ARC, 1982. Five-page biography of Barton includes details and main events of her life.

———, *The International Red Cross*. American Red Cross pamphlet 1316. Washington, DC: ARC, 1987. Summarizes world mission of the organization.

Clara Barton, *The Red Cross: A History of This Remarkable International Movement in the Interest of Humanity*. New York: American National Red Cross, 1898. Long, detailed account containing many entire reports, audits, addresses, and lists.

William E. Barton, *The Life of Clara Barton*. 2 vols. Boston: Houghton Mifflin, 1922. Style is difficult but provides detailed picture.

Vince Beiser, "Kasandra Milne: Compassion Under Fire," *Maclean's*, December 27, 1993. Interview with a Red Cross volunteer.

John S. Blay, *After the Civil War: A Pictorial Profile of America from 1865 to 1900*. New York: Bonanza Books, 1960. Indexed, topical illustrations of reconstruction, everyday life, politics, capital and labor, the arts, progress and growth, the frontier, and empire building from contemporary sources.

Percy H. Epler, *The Life of Clara Barton*. New York: Macmillan, 1917. Detailed account of Barton's life and career by one of her authorized biographers.

Joel Chandler Harris, "The Sea Island Hurricanes: The Relief," *Scribner's Magazine*, March 1894. Comprehensive coverage of damage done, the area, and the people, with a good sprinkling of Harris's skillful renditions of the dialect of these isolated coastal islands.

Robert Leckie, *The Wars of America*. New York: Harper & Row, 1981. Revised and updated from edition of 1948. Lively and readable political accounts. Politics and issues rather than chronology. Index.

Maurice Matloff, ed., *The Civil War: A Concise History of the War Between the States*. Adapted from *American Military History*. Illustrated by John W. Howard. New York: McKay, 1978. Includes portraits from the Picture Collection of the New York Public Library.

"The Red Cross Under Fire," *World Press Review*, June 1992. Analysis of Red Cross neutrality in the 1990s.

Ishbel Ross, *Angel of the Battlefield: The Life of Clara Barton*. New York: Harper & Brothers, 1956. Full-length biography, suitable for excellent readers, with many details about the famous personages with whom Clara Barton worked. Many photos.

"Samaritan in Somalia," *People*, December 28, 1993. Portrait of Red Cross worker Mary Taylor.

Richard Wheeler, ed., *Sherman's March*. New York: Crowell, 1979. Diaries telling of a campaign that helped defeat the Confederacy.

Blanche Colton Williams, *Clara Barton: Daughter of Destiny*. Philadelphia: Lippincott, 1941. Full-scale biography using many primary sources but providing no documentation. Written after Barton's diaries were found. Several appendices. Index.

Charles Sumner Young, *Clara Barton: A Centenary Tribute*. Boston: Richard G. Badger/Gorham Press, 1922. Brief sketches. Not chronological. Does not cite sources.

Index

Picture Credits

Cover photo: Library of Congress

American Red Cross, 9, 20, 32, 70

Archive Photos, 24 (bottom), 40

The Bettmann Archive, 26, 31 (top), 35, 37, 47, 51, 55 (bottom), 68, 71, 73, 80, 85 (bottom), 99

Library of Congress, 11 (both), 12, 13, 16, 19, 22, 27, 28, 29, 41 (bottom), 43, 44, 49, 53, 55 (top), 60, 63, 64, 67, 77, 83

84 (both), 85 (top), 86 (bottom), 87, 89, 90, 93, 96, 97

National Archives, 31 (bottom), 38, 41 (top), 46

Reuters/Bettmann, 101

Stock Montage, 10, 24 (top), 33, 52, 54 (both), 82, 94

UPI/Bettmann, 74 (both), 86 (top), 91, 92

About the Author

Rafael Tilton, Ph.D., is an educator, editor, and writer who lives and works in rural Montana. Tilton brought a spirit of political activism, involvement in global issues, and a family tradition of nonviolence to this study of Clara Barton. Barton's long life, physical strength under stress, and several careers challenge the imagination of this teacher who also has worked in nursing homes, food service, and newspaper offices. Several women on the maternal side of the Tilton family were named for the famous American who brought the Red Cross to the United States.